The Colour of Gold

To Debbie
&
Adriane   May 5/99.

Margaret McKirdy-

The Colour of Gold

Margaret McKirdy

CAITLIN PRESS
Box 2387, Stn.B
Prince George, BC
V2N 2S6

Caitlin Press Inc.
Box 2387
Station B
Prince George, BC
V2N 2S6

Caitlin Press acknowledges the support of the Canada Council for the Arts for our publishing program. Similiarly, we acknowledge the support of the Arts Council of British Columbia.

Cover design by Gaye Hammond.
Page design and output by David Lee Communications.
Edited by A--Z Wordsmith.
Map on page 8 by Lionheart Graphics.
Printed in Canada by Webcom Ltd.

Canadian cataloguing in publication data

McKirdy, Margaret, 1922–
The Colour of Gold

Includes photos and index
ISBN 0-920576-66-4

1. MacCauley, Adelaide. 2. Trials(Murder)—Britsh Columbia—Golden
3. Metis—British Columbia—Biography. I. Title
HV6535.C33G64 1997   346.15'23'092   C97-910191-3

Dedication

To my sister, Laurel Baird,
who from this book's inception
guided my faltering steps.

Acknowledgments

This book is the direct result of a day's browsing, four years ago, through the records in the Provincial Archives, Victoria. I happened on a letter to the Attorney-General concerning the death of Alexander McCaulay, at Swift Current Creek, near Mt. Robson, in the Rocky Mountains. Thanks to the diligence of David Mattison, Reference Archivist, and Brent McBride, Reference Services, who uncovered much material for a story about the first Supreme Court Trial in Golden, B.C. Thanks also to the Golden and District Historic Society, the diligence of the curator of their museum, Colleen Torrence, and the society's published history, Golden Memories. They contributed an equal amount of material.

Information generously supplied by the following archives and people completed my store of archival references:

Valemount and District Historic Society, Shirley Klettl and Ishbel Cochrane; Jasper and District Historic Society, Glenda Cornforth, Tom Peterson, and Dale Portman; Glenbow Archives, Calgary, Alberta; Whyte Museum of the Canadian Rockies, Banff, Alberta; National Archives of Canada, Ottawa; Atmospheric Environment Service, Environment Canada; Canadian Pacific Archives, Montreal.

I would also like to thank Rene Nunweiler for patient reading and insightful comments, Natalie Olson for same, and Stephani Judy for editing suggestions early in the writing; and Lon Nunweiler for teaching me to master my ornery computer.

Thanks to: Dr. David and Mrs. Jane Norwell for information including medical practices at the turn of the century; to

Angus McKirdy, Liz Norwell, Nannette Mosley, Edna Howard, Catherine Hiroe, Evelyn Hart, and Berna Paquette for information about life on the trail, the native language and culture, and so forth; to Ralph Wass for deciphering hand written documents; and to Lyle Norlander for locating the site of McCaulay's grave.

The books I have consulted, all of which contributed something, are too numerous to mention, however, the following deserve special consideration: *The First Métis, A New Nation*, by Dr. Anne Anderson; *Golden Memories*, by the Golden and District Historic Society; *The Golden Era*, Golden's newspaper of the turn of the century; *Riel and the Rebellion, 1885 Reconsidered*, by Thomas Flanagan; *Exploitation of Métis Lands*, by Emile Pelletier; and *Portraits of the Premiers*, by S. W. Jackman.

And finally, thanks to Cynthia Wilson for prodding me to flesh out the story, and to Liz Jones for careful editing and for supplying the threads that joined two diverse stories (one of the incidents near Mount Robson, the other of the hearings and trial in Golden) into a cohesive unit.

For the help from others along the way, I am truly grateful.

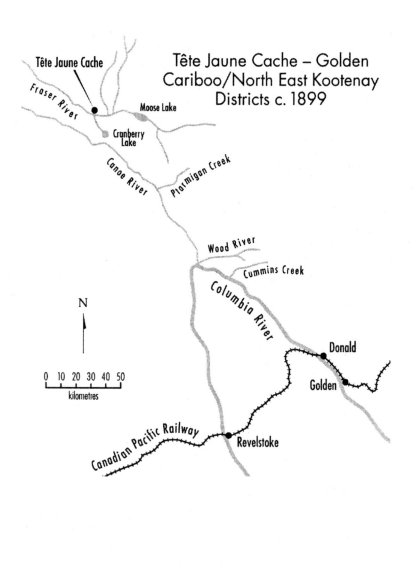

Tête Jaune Cache – Golden
Cariboo/North East Kootenay
Districts c. 1899

Chapter I

On a clear June morning, Clara Keller, tall, gaunt, and somewhat stooped, stood and gazed out of the window of her son's house at the white peaks cradling Salt Lake City. At the insistence of her granddaughter, she had recently had her hair styled for the first time in her life. Once a tediously braided bun, her hair now framed her face in soft white curls that gave her a new sense of freedom and a longing for adventure. Her eyes ranged northward following the Rocky Mountains until they disappeared into a seeming infinity.

Somewhere there, somewhere she had never gone, her brother Percy had looked out onto the same mountain range. He had felt the same sun shine overhead, and watched the same moon rise and set. The same sky arched above. He lived, and he died. He had never followed that mountain range south again, nor had any of the family wandered north. Clara was eleven years old when she had last seen her brother, Percy.

Clara had attended the burial of Mama and Papa. She had placed fresh flowers on their graves and read the gravestones that guarded them. She married, had a long and fairly happy life, and raised a family who cherished her. Her grandchildren had grown and now brought their children to visit. Soon, her son Alan's eldest grandchild would be a mother. Her life had been full, but over the recent years, she had attended the burial of eleven of her brothers and sisters. She had buried her husband and two of her children. None of her family knew Percy. None had seen the place where he lived out his life. None had placed a stone to mark his falling.

Clara felt the arm embrace her shoulder. "What is it Mama," Alan said. "What is the matter?"

"It's Percy," Clara said. "I feel him in the room here. He came to me in my dream again last night. When he saw me he waved and I could see the sparkle in his brown eyes as he ran toward me. I expected him to pick me up and swing me in the air the way he did so long ago. Somehow, I just can't stop thinking of him. I don't know what he is trying to tell me."

Clara's brother Percy was born in 1858. An older son in a large family, he left home at nineteen to prospect for gold. He travelled through California, Colorado, Utah, Idaho, and Washington, and then he disappeared into Canada. The last letter Clara had from him was postmarked Beavermouth, British Columbia. This June morning was the centennial of his birth.

"Neither of us have ever been to Canada. It's time we went. I'll sit down today and write the postmaster at Beavermouth," Alan said giving his mother a hug. "Maybe, someone there remembers Percy. Maybe someone knows where he lived and where he died. I would love to go with you to those places. We can follow his trail of adventure. If we can find where he is buried and when he died, you can place a gravestone over him. You can put Uncle Percy to rest."

Dr. Alan Keller put pen to paper then mailed his missive. "I've thrown my query to the winds," he told his mother. "And what will the winds return?"

Short weeks later, a letter arrived from Victoria, British Columbia.

"Dearest Clara," they read, "The postmaster at Beavermouth forwarded your letter to me. I am very much alive, and I am celebrating my centennial along with British Columbia. There is nothing wrong with me. I've never known so much comfort in my life. People here are so kind to me, but I think of you often. Could you send me pictures of yourself and of your family? Do you have grandchildren? I would love to see pictures of them, and to hear what all the family are doing. Ever since I received Alan's letter, I sit and think about you and about all of the family. Please write as soon as you can and tell me about everyone. Love, Percy."

❖

Percy had stood watching for the arrival of his sister for over an hour. He had become tired and confused. His hands shook on his supporting canes. When he saw a man and a woman approaching, his mind suddenly slipped back over eighty years.

What he saw—what he thought he saw—was his Grandma rushing forward. He saw Papa trailing behind. Percy stood riveted, speechless.

"Percy!" the woman called.

"Gra . . . " and just in time, "Clara!" Percy answered. "My darling Clara!"

Percy's visitors stayed for a month while Percy and Clara relived the eighty years they had been lost to each other. Clara had brought albums of pictures, clippings from small town newspapers, and bundles of letters, both recent and yellow with age. Percy learned of a hundred of his kin scattered throughout the western states. He examined pictures, learned of marriages, births and deaths, of health, endeavour, success, of failure, crippling illness, diphtheria, scarlet fever, small pox, mountain fever, tuberculosis, child bed fever, pneumonia, accident, and even murder.

"I keep wanting to call you Uncle Peter," Alan interrupted. "You remind me so of Uncle Peter. But you're not surrounded by children. Uncle Peter loved his grandchildren, and he had dozens of them. Did you never marry?"

"Well, I planned to often enough," Percy laughed. "When I left home, I promised Annie I would make my fortune and return for her. Remember Annie, Clara?"

"Annie didn't wait for you," Clara responded, smiling. "She married Johnny Black within the year."

"There weren't many girls to be found in the places where I searched for gold, but there were some. There was a lovely girl with flaxen braids in California. Her name just doesn't come to mind. And then, Dollie, the merry-eyed brunette in Utah, and

Katie, the lithe young redhead in Idaho. I wonder if any of them are still waiting. I never did find that fortune, but I loved them all dearly."

"Then, there was Adelaide," Percy continued quietly. "She disappeared. I never did know where though I searched for her for years."

Percy looked off into the distance and his eyes became glazed. "Adelaide," he said. "Adelaide. She called me—Kid." Gazing inward, he travelled back through time and over the miles.

In the early spring of 1899, Alex McCaulay, a Métis trapper, together with Adelaide and Mosie, his Cree wife and son, had been hunting along the Athabasca River south of Henry House. They were returning with a moose, quartered and on the pack horses, when Jim Hughes came riding to meet them. Adelaide watched his horse approach at a slow walk. She saw Hughes' cold eyes sweep over them. Minutes passed as he came closer, and she noted the deep wine cast of his face, watched his sour expression, felt the brute power in his broad figure. He eyed Alex. She remembered an official who once came to the trading post and didn't give much for their furs.

As they met and reined in, Hughes spoke abruptly. "They tell me you ride through the mountains."

"Ehe," Alex replied. His eyes were drawn to Hughes' saddle.

"Ever heard about gold in Swift Current Creek?" Hughes continued.

"Some."

"I see you like that saddle," Hughes remarked.

"Ehe," Alex said. "It's a beauty."

"Well it's yours, if you take me there."

Adelaide understood few of the English words. She saw Alex smile and nod in agreement, and her slim figure tensed. She watched and listened, as alert as a doe that senses danger.

Just as Hughes turned to leave, Mosie's horse shied and threw him to the ground.

Mother and father rushed to Mosie who lay moaning on the ground. As Adelaide comforted him and checked for injury, Alex rode after and caught the horse.

When they turned back to Hughes, he was gone. They saw him disappearing in the distance.

Before Hughes had joined them, Adelaide's brown eyes had been merry; her voice lilted as she joked with Alex and Mosie. Later when she comforted Mosie, her eyes were soft, her voice tender.

Now, her eyes flashed black, her jaw set, and her black braid swung as she straightened. She exploded in anger. "We won't go to the mountains with him!"

"I'm a guide Adelaide," Alex laughed. "We don't need to like the guy. We just get him there. We can trap beaver," he reasoned.

Adelaide looked at her strong young husband. She saw his confidence, and slowly her confidence rose and her fears evaporated.

Alex, Adelaide, and Mosie rode back to Henry House Flats. When they planned the hunting trip, Alex had said, "Mosie should go with us. He should learn to handle a horse, and to read the signs of the forest, and to hunt. Mary should stay with Kohkum."

As they rode into the camp, nieces, nephews, and cousins with Mary in tow ran to meet them. A young cousin lifted Mary up onto Adelaide's horse, and she rode with her mother to the cabin.

Before they could leave with Hughes, Adelaide needed to cure the moose meat. Alex unpacked the horses and dropped the meat near Kohkum's cabin. Kohkum (Adelaide's grand-mother), Adelaide's sister and her cousins, together with their daughters, came to help.

Women and girls gathered dry wood and poles. They lit a fire that would make deep coals with plenty of heat to cook the head and the budding antlers. Then, the women used the poles to make a drying rack, and were ready to cut the meat.

They cut carefully, following around until they had big thin sheets of meat which they hung on the rack to dry. Women and girls, from the oldest to the youngest, contributed what help they could.

"You better learn to handle that knife good," Adelaide said to her little cousin. "Someday you'll have a husband, and he'll give you a new baby every year. You got to learn to look after things."

The little girl bent seriously to her task, and Adelaide smiled.

Adelaide laid the moose head in the fire, turned it to singe the hair, pulled it out, and scraped off the singed hair. She cut out the brain and laid it aside to use when she tanned the hide. The antlers were in velvet and would make horn butter. She cut them off and would cook them in the coals later. The people would slice off the burnt velvet and eat the horn butter spreading it on dried meat. When she had the head prepared, she braced a pole over the fire and hung the moose head by a rawhide rope.

Kohkum took over the task of watching the head while it cooked. She sat, drank tea, and turned the head so that it cooked evenly. She drank tea, and the children came.

"Tell us a story," the children cried. "Tell us a story about our people."

This was the story Kohkum told them:

A long time ago, it was. Some of the people came in canoes. The fur traders wished to come to the mountains, and they asked the people to bring them. The people brought the fur traders in the boats. Up the rivers, they paddled. From the good weather season until the trees were bare, they paddled and they portaged. They brought the fur traders. That was a long time ago. When *Musom* was a little boy, he was told by his grandfather, and maybe before that even. The people were Iroquois then. They were strong, and they travelled with canoes, big canoes. Not with horses like now, only with canoes.

In the mountains they followed the rivers. They found the way through the mountains. Through the mountains to the big rivers. Where we go now, they went. They went and they trapped mink and marten, bears too, and beaver. They traded those to the fur traders, and they fished. Some of the Iroquois married with the Shuswap, and they brought the Shuswap back through the mountains.

After that, not so long ago as the Iroquois. Kohkum was a young girl then. The people came from the Red River. The people came from the Red River because the buffalo were all gone. The people had horses for to hunt the buffalo. They came with horses. Not canoes. Only horses.

Gabriel came from the Red River, and he brought his fiddle. He made the bow dance on the strings, and we danced. Oh! How we danced! Gabriel fiddled faster and faster, and we danced. No matter how fast Gabriel played, me and Musom danced. Some of the people got tired and fell to the ground, but we danced!

The people from the Red River were mostly Cree and French. Mostly, they were Cree and French. The Iroquois married with them. Sometimes they married with white men. These were the people, the Métis, the people who danced to the fiddle or the drum. Whatever it was, we danced.

But those people are gone now. Some of the people died with the coughing sickness. Many of the people died with the coughing. Some with the red spots, they died.

Now the people speak Cree. Only Cree, not Iroquois, not Shuswap, only Cree. And they ride horses. Mostly they ride horses.

The children listened attentively as Kohkum's voice changed from merry to sad. Then, one boy grabbed two sticks, one the fiddle and one the bow. "Dance Kohkum," he said. As he drew the bow across, he sang:

"*Kispin ke sagien*
Saymuk Koshamin.

If you like me, come kiss me," he sang.

The children all jumped up and danced about the fire.

While her skilled helpers cut the rest of the meat, and Kohkum watched the head, Adelaide worked with the hide. She made a frame with sturdy poles, and using rawhide strips, laced the hide to the frame and stretched it till it was tight. With her *mihkehkwun*, she scraped gristle, fat, and bits of muscle from every inch of the hide. Then, she hung the hide behind the cabin.

"You chase away them damn squirrels," Adelaide said as she patted Kohkum's dog. "You gotta earn your keep just like everybody." She left the hide to dry, and the dog lay next to it daring the squirrels to come near.

When the meat was all cut and on the rack, the head was nearly cooked, Alex played the drums, and the neighbours came from up, down, and across the river.

One of the woman made bannock, mixing it in the flour sack. She opened the sack, mixed some salt and baking powder into the flour, and made a well with her hand. Into the well she poured water, mixed water and flour, and patted the dough into cakes. She greased the hot fry pan with marrow, set it on the hot coals, added the cakes of bannock, and soon the meal was ready.

The women, their men, and the children had a feast. They ate the moose nose, the eyes, the tongue, and the meat from the cheeks. They ate the bannock, and they drank the tea, and it was good.

Gabriel's grandson played the fiddle, and they danced, and they sang. Alex and Adelaide's feet flew as they danced. Mosie danced with his young cousin while Mary bounced to the music. For a few brief minutes Musom and Kohkum danced the wild dance of their youth. One by one the children fell asleep, and their mothers laid them on Kohkum's bed or on a blanket or a hide in the corner, and rejoined the dancers. All of it was good.

When Adelaide left with Alex to travel through the Yellowhead Pass, Kohkum was left in charge of the meat and the hide. She watched during the day, and her dog guarded at night until the meat was completely dry, and then she took it into her cabin.

In her small cabin, she had a fireplace of mud and stones, and her bed of furs, hides, and blankets. She had a table and chairs—chairs with woven rawhide seats—which had been made by some forgotten ancestor of Musom. She did not always sit on a chair. When she sewed, she sat on the floor. When people came, when strangers came, they sat on the chairs. Then she sat on a chair, too.

Kohkum had a shelf by the fireplace for baking powder, salt, dried herbs, and matches. Her cooking pot, tea pail, griddle, and damp clothes hung from pegs. Away from the fireplace, was another shelf for the water pail, dipper, and wash basin. Near that she had a grub box where sugar, flour, beans, rice, and tea were kept free from mice and other rodents. Kohkum folded the dried meat tightly and stuffed it into sugar sacks which she dropped into the grub box. The meat would feed herself, Alex and his family, all Kohkum's children, her grandchildren, and whoever else was hungry.

Early the next morning Kohkum went out to begin curing the hide. With her *matahikun*, she scraped off the fur and shaved the thick skin. She tapped the taut hide with her fingertips. The sound told her which places were thick, which thin. As she worked, the shavings fell to the ground, and her dog licked them up. This was the dog's reward for keeping squirrels and wild prowlers away from hide and meat.

Kohkum worked in the way her mother had taught her, the same way her mother's mother before her had worked. When she had the hide trimmed so it was even, not thick and thin, she put on moose brain and rubbed in a circular motion, over and over, round and round. The sun helped her make the hide soft and pliable. If the day was cloudy, she often tired before the job was done. At those times, she took the hide from the frame, rolled it into a small bundle, and let the oil from the brain do the work.

When the hide was pliable, she immersed the bundle of hide in a tub of water and left it to soak. Now, she needed strong arms and a strong back to help her. She fetched her daughter and her sister's daughter. They took the hide and twisted it on a stick; round and round they twisted it until it was tight and the water was out.

While the young women wrung the water from the hide, Kohkum built a fire with some green and some rotted wood; she wanted smoke and only a little flame. Her daughter and her sister's daughter stretched the hide above the flame and waved it up and down, and the smoke curled around. They waved it, never stopping, not stopping till the hide was dry. When Kohkum was young, she and her sister did this, but because she was old now, her daughter and her sister's daughter did it.

When the hide was dry, the young women left her to do the rest. She nailed both ends of a wire to the wall so that it formed a circle. Then she inserted the hide into the circle and pulled it back and forth through the loop, working on each area until it was soft. The hard spots she rubbed between her fingers, and it seemed no time until it was all soft. Long ago, before the trade stores, the women had no wire, and they chewed the hide to make it soft. Her teeth were worn to the gums. The women, now, didn't want to wear their teeth away, and she had learned to use the wire, too.

When the hide was soft enough, Kohkum built a small fire, a small smouldering fire. She wanted no flame, only thick smoke. She fashioned the hide into a bag on a frame and held it so the smoke went into the pouch. In time, the hide turned to a golden colour, like the sun in a thick smoke. The hide was ready. She could make moccasins, leggings, and shirts, whatever the hide fit.

She would make moccasins like she made for Musom. For Musom she decorated the moccasins with red blanket cloth, beads, quills from the porcupine, fur and tails from the squirrels. How those moccasins flew when Musom danced! She would make moccasins for Mosie. Already his feet could fly when he danced.

From the small pieces of hide, she would make fringes for shirt and leggings. She would waste nothing, not even time: she would sew in the winter when there were no berries to pick.

Alex, Adelaide and their children had left the next morning after the meat was cut. They rode for two days to where Hughes was staying, and then they waited. Alex's family was ready to leave because Hughes had told Alex he wanted to go right away, but Hughes made them wait for three days.

I could have stayed and helped Kohkum, Adelaide thought. I could have done the hard work, but Hughes must be the boss, and we must wait.

Finally, Hughes joined them, and they were on their way west through the Yellowhead Pass. Although the snow had melted and the ground was bare in the open, snow coated the floor of the forest and the shaded slope of the hills; frost firmed the sloughs and ice coated the rocky slopes. They followed the low winter trail rather than attempting to navigate through the icy cliffs. The spring freshet was still weeks away; hence, the rivers were shallow and easily forded, but water splashed up and as they travelled on, the wind penetrated damp clothing and left them, after a short day's ride, chilled. The children grew cranky, and when they stopped, the family was ready for the comfort of camp.

While Adelaide set up camp beside a stream, made bannock, and tended the children, Alex unpacked the horses and checked their feet which, unshod, were easily bruised by the rocky terrain. Alex then put the horses to pasture. Winter grass afforded little nutrition so the horses needed a long night to graze. They also needed hours to rest tender feet.

Alex went along the creek, set traps, and came back with crow's eggs for the evening meal. Later, he would hunt until dark. Season, weather, terrain, availability of food, and pasture shaped their day.

Hughes, in the meantime, gave his horses oats, checked their shod feet, lit a fire, cooked rice and bacon, and boiled tea. He then checked the stream for gold, found no colour, and was ready to move on, to travel until dusk. When Alex shook his head saying there was no pasture ahead, Hughes cursed and walked away.

Later in the evening, Alex checked his traps and found two beaver. Adelaide quickly skinned out the beaver, gutted the carcasses, and hung them to dry. Dried beaver meat was good for when they travelled. While Adelaide skinned the beaver, Alex cut two willow branches, stripped the bark from them, and proceeded to lace the hides onto a circular willow frame with the strips of bark.

Hughes, who sat sullenly by his fire drinking tea, came wandering over. "Those are my hides," he said.

"Why? Did you catch them?" Alex asked.

"Stupid! I gave you a saddle. You are working for me!"

"I must be stupid. Is that how you catch beaver?" Alex snorted.

"If I have to kill you, I'll have those beaver!"

Alex, lean and young, assessed Hughes' powerful bulk, then retorted, "Well, kill me now!"

Hughes stomped away into his tent. He did not come out again that evening, nor did he and Alex speak the next day.

Later, Adelaide remembered how Hughes spoke to Alex in English, but to her and the children not at all. When Hughes was around, Adelaide felt constantly uneasy. As Alex and the children slept, Adelaide recalled the endless disagreements that erupted, again and again, over anything, or over nothing. Sometimes Hughes and Alex forgot their differences and seemed the best of friends, and then for no reason that she could see, Hughes was angry again. Her mind in a turmoil, Adelaide slept. She slept and she dreamed.

Chapter II

Just before the day began to break, a *wihtikow* entered the teepee. A mutilated face with lips gnawed away stared with hungry eyes. Bare teeth grimaced in a lipless mouth. The wihtikow's gaunt figure crept noiselessly closer. A dark mass moved before it. The wihtikow sunk ever lower. Eyes scanned from every shadowy corner, every hidden crevice. The face, the lipless face of Hughes ogled her, her breasts, her legs, her thighs; his stealthy eyes watched her! The wihtikow crept closer, ever closer. The face, the face of Hughes—Hughes, once fleshy, now gaunt, cadaverous—turned to Alex, sniffed the air, snarled; bared teeth slobbered hungrily. Feral eyes devoured Alex.

She tried to move, to reach for her knife. Her limbs froze. Hughes was almost upon them, upon Alex.

She opened her mouth! Screamed! No voice came. She jerked awake.

Hughes, the wihtikow, vanished.

Shaking, she pulled the children to her, and placed herself between Alex and the entry. She began to rock, and swaying back and forth, she emitted a mournful chant.

Chapter III

When she told Alex about the wihtikow, he was angry. "Hughes is not a wihtikow," he said. "There are no wihtikows! You dreamt!" He fingered the medallion hanging at his neck. Adelaide said nothing.

Later on the trail, Adelaide rode quietly. Mosie had begged to ride with her, so she had both children. She clicked her tongue, and her horse, Pinto, broke into a trot.

When Alex and Hughes talked, Adelaide understood some of what they said. She knew some of the English words that Alex used, but she was tired of listening. Out of earshot, she reined Pinto to a walk, and as they continued on, she shook off her foreboding.

She saw deer tracks and spoke to the children in Cree, "See! A deer and fawn went this way."

Sun glistened on the stream. New young buds of colt's foot and mountain lily burst from the soil. A gentle breeze carried the song of robin, the chatter of junco, the far off call of the varied thrush, the rippling of water on rocks, and the perfumes of the forest. The spirits of nature mingled with those of the riders.

Adelaide pointed to more tracks, still moist, on the trail ahead. "See? The deer? Her baby? We scared them," she whispered.

Alex joined them, and as the family rode, the sun warmed them, and the breeze cooled. Mary reached up searching for her mother's breast, and Adelaide let her nurse as they rode. Patches of melting snow filled the hollows along the trail, snow melted among the bushes and in the shaded areas and snow on the sharp peaks of the Rocky Mountains glistened.

"In one moon," Alex said, "beaver season is over. We will ride back to Henry House. No more Hughes," Alex promised.

Adelaide warmed to Alex's flashing smile. She thought about this trip in reverse without Hughes to interfere. They would pause a dozen times. The pleasure would stay with them for the whole of the summer, and she said, "It will be good to be just us again, to travel on and see Kohkum again—and our brothers, and sisters, and cousins."

"Ehe," said Mosie.

Mary smiled contentedly. Adelaide nestled her down onto the horse and held her as she dozed.

Adelaide thought about home. In early summer, the people returned from trap lines. There would be feasting and dancing. Adelaide would talk, and talk, and talk with other women.

When they travelled, Alex talked to everyone, but Adelaide talked only to the Cree; often, that was only Alex and the children. But it was a beautiful day. Soon they would travel home to friends.

Hughes was out of sight.

As they jogged along, Alex sang,

"And I will love thee still, my dear,

Till a' the seas gang dry."

The children watched and listened to their father with rapt adoration.

Suddenly, Alex smelled a wood fire, saw smoke curl from the riverside. People! Alex silenced his song.

Adelaide, watching his tension rise, knew he rehearsed what he would say and do. Alex doesn't know whether he is Indian or white, she mused. His slim figure, like her own, looked Indian enough, and his skin was almost as dark as hers. He was dressed in buckskin, and she had beaded his fringed jacket and his moccasins. His face, like many Indians, was whisker free. But he had told her about his father, about Scotland, about how he longed to see that country.

Musom's papa was white, she concluded, but I am not. She sighed for Alex.

As they approached the camp, they saw the combination of tents and teepees, woven garb and moose hide. The people were Métis. Alex relaxed.

Alex had learned languages at his father's side. He had been quicker to pick up on languages than his father, and he knew a few words in many native tongues as well as English and French. He spoke to everyone. A wave, a simple hello, or 'bon jour' was enough to start a conversation. From there, with words garnered from a mixture of languages, mostly Cree, together with pointing and gestures, he communicated. But Adelaide knew that Alex felt comfortable only with the Métis.

These people were on their way home from trapping. Adelaide noted the Cree moccasins, the Cree designs of beading. She brightened. While Alex talked to the men, she turned to the women.

"You got new baby," she said to a young woman.

"New last moon," the woman answered. She held the baby up for mother and children to admire.

Mosie and Mary, who had roused at the sound of strange voices, reached out and touched the baby's fingers and cheek. They murmured softly. Their eyes turned from the baby to the other children, and then to Adelaide.

They were about to dismount when Hughes, who had stopped to check his horses' packs, rode up and sat aloof, surveying his surroundings.

"Let's get t' hell out of here," he said to Alex.

Adelaide listened. Although she did not understand many of the words, the angry tone translated. She saw Alex look at his new friends and shrug.

As they continued on their way, Adelaide fumed. She wanted to stop for the day. Had they been on their own, she knew that they would have. But, she thought, Hughes talks to his horses as she would to respected elders. She thought of the grain he fed them. When Mosie took a handful, just to taste,

Hughes lunged at him and bellowed, "Get out of there, you little bastard."

Adelaide knew that, had Hughes not depended on Alex to find his way, Mosie would have been booted. She thought about the marten.

When Hughes checked, there was a marten, caught by a paw, in the beaver trap. The hair was scrubbed bare from its belly and the tits were swollen with milk. Alex would have set it free, but Hughes brained it with a club and chucked it into the river.

Adelaide tried to find the orphaned babies, but she couldn't. She shrugged angrily. Soon we will go to our own people, she thought.

As they left the Athabasca River to travel up the Miette, the trail deteriorated rapidly. The horses skirted around or jumped over fallen timber. Pack horses forked out in all directions, and Alex and Hughes chased after them. Sometimes, one or the other jumped from his horse to catch a stray by the halter and steer it back onto the trail.

Adelaide spent much of the day leading her horse, carrying Mary, and encouraging Mosie to scramble ahead or keep to her side. Six times during the day, they mounted the horse and forded the rocky stream. The sun had set behind the mountains before they found sparse pasture and could stop for the night.

Adelaide quickly kindled a fire and made bannock. Alex caught a small trout, and Adelaide fried it and fed the children before they fell exhausted, onto a hide blanket where they slept while Alex and Adelaide ate. While Adelaide erected the teepee, made a bed of boughs, and transferred the sleeping children to it, Alex unpacked the horses and hung what he could to dry.

The second day's travel along the Miette was no better than the first, but at the end of that day, they came upon a lush pasture. When they stopped for the night, Hughes fed grain to all his horses and let them go.

"Maybe, better hobble one," Alex suggested. "They wander away."

"If you treated your horses right," Hughes barked, "They'd stay around like mine do."

Alex and Adelaide silently made camp and fed the children the grouse Alex had shot. Hughes erected his tent a short distance away. Whenever Alex guided anyone, he shot game and fished, but they supplied the rest of the grub. Hughes did at first, but before they had travelled two days, he began to eat alone and hoard his supplies.

Adelaide bristled, but Alex laughed. "We've lived off the land before," he said. "We can do it again. Let's forget it. We'll be rid of Hughes in no time."

When Alex caught a beaver, Adelaide gutted the carcass, stuffed it with herbs and roots, placed it in her cast iron cooking pot, and fitted the cast iron lid. She then dug a hole beside the campfire, scraped half of the coals into the hole, placed the pot in the hole, scraped the remainder of the coals around it, and built another fire on top. The beaver would be their food for the next day. The meat was rich and fat so they didn't eat much, only a little bit with bannock.

She stretched the pelt and hung it from a teepee pole. When they moved on Alex would hang it on the side of the packsaddle.

As they continued to travel, they left the Miette River behind them. The sun shone as they rode along at a leisurely pace; they didn't realize they had crossed the divide until they noticed the streams flowed with them. Towards evening, they came upon pasture by a lake, a blue gem set among green timber and white capped peaks.

During the night, clouds drifted in, and when they woke, they stepped out into a blanket of snow. Huge flakes of wet snow settled on them.

Alex decided it was not a day to travel. He told Hughes about the hard day's travel ahead through the forest that surrounded the lake. Alex told him about the necessity to travel on to Moose Lake before they reached pasture. He explained that, with another day's rest, the horses would be better prepared.

Hughes fumed. "Is the trail bad?" he asked, "Or are you just too lazy?"

None the less, Alex stayed, and Hughes was forced to wait until the following day when they resumed their travel and skirted Moose Lake. They avoided the bush as much as they could by riding along the lake shore and on the compact snow that covered the frozen lake. The end of a long day brought them out onto a large, pleasant meadow beyond the lake, and here, they camped.

Overnight, the sky cleared, and they woke to a see brilliant sun peeking above the mountains, a perfect day to lay over, dry their clothes, and replenish the larder. Because they did so, they again faced a sullen Hughes. However, prospectors going out camped near, and Hughes kept his temper in check.

Alex traded with the prospectors, a bear hide for their extra flour. Alex and Adelaide had left the moose with Kohkum to dry, but on their way, Alex had shot a bear. The hide was prime; the carcass, from hibernation, was thin, and the meat stringy but edible. He shot small game and birds, gathered eggs, and caught fish. All these Adelaide cooked. She sometimes buried the meat in the coals as she had the beaver. At other times she fried the fish or boiled meat with spring shoots of colt's foot, lily bulbs, Indian potato, or whatever herbs she found.

Now, she could add flour to make a stew. She made bannock to complete the meal and saved a few pieces for the children to munch when they travelled. They needed this because they did not stop to eat during the day.

Although Hughes had oats for his horses, Alex had none. Spring growth in the pasture lands had not begun, and Alex's horses, dependent entirely on winter grass, required more time to feed.

"Jesus! You spend a lot of time camping," Hughes fumed.

"My family, they like to eat." Alex scarcely hid his amusement.

The next morning when they were ready to leave, Hughes' horses were nowhere in sight. "Don't see no horses," was Alex's laconic comment.

"They're just beyond that ridge," Hughes replied tersely.

Alex reset his traps, caught two beaver, and was skinning one when Hughes returned at noon.

Hughes rode up. "Why in hell aren't you ready? You've had time enough!"

"Ehe," said Alex. "You found your horses, anahow."

"Mind your own business, you bloody breed," Hughes snapped.

"You've called me a breed often enough!" Alex snapped back.

"What you going to do about it? I'll make mincemeat out of you!" Hughes threatened. The children began to cry. Adelaide saw Hughes' menacing pose, saw his feet dance just a bit, watched his eyes. Hughes was old; older than Alex. He was thick around the middle, but Hughes had been a fighter.

"*Qwigo! Muqway gesgetum.*" Adelaide murmured to Alex. "That's enough! He knows nothing! *Astum,*" Adelaide said as she folded her babies in her arms. "Come away from Hughes."

Alex looked at his family, sighed, and walked away from Hughes. Throughout the day Alex and Hughes treated each other curtly, but by the next morning, Alex had shrugged off his pique. Hughes, however, followed at a distance, approaching Alex only to demand information or assistance.

Adelaide enjoyed the distance created by Hughes, and the opportunity to be a family again. As they neared Mount Robson, the spirits of home fell behind, and Adelaide felt new spirits join them. Spirits of water murmuring over rocks, of bursting new growth, of rustling leaves, of flitting camp robbers—all that day, she felt their presence. The mountains and the spirits enfolded her, the mother with her family.

Chapter IV

As she made camp near the mouth of Swift Current Creek, Adelaide's appearance was that of a slim young girl. Her long hair was tied back with a leather thong. Her calico dress reached to her ankles, and a plaid shawl covered her shoulders. She had forgotten Hughes. She opened the shell case and tore a match from the block of Chinese matches that Alex had bought at the trading post. Flames licked the brown leaves and twigs and curled about the logs. She hummed softly. Through the murmur of the breeze and the thunder of water over rocks, she heard the spirit of the drums, the drums that her tribe danced to, would dance to again this summer. "Hay-ya, hay-ya, hay-ya, hay!"

Suddenly, Hughes brushed against her. Adelaide shuddered, recoiled, and stared. She silenced her chant, and bent to her task.

Hughes wheeled about and strode over to Alex. "Where's the gold," he asked.

"What gold?" Alex replied. "I haven't seen no gold."

"You stupid breed," Hughes retorted as he stomped away.

Adelaide gathered firewood, and in minutes, had the fire blazing. She fetched water for tea. The only words she understood from the conversation were "stupid breed." Stupid breed, dirty breed, filthy Indian, and dumb clooch; she had heard them all before.

Swift Current Creek, the wildest stream they encountered on this trip, roiled, foamed, and tumbled against huge boulders. The water gouged the banks. From her campfire beside the stream, Adelaide watched a root, torn from the banks, ride the wild rapids. It twisted and turned, submerged and surfaced, finally to lodge behind a boulder. Her anger melted away as she finished preparing the meal.

Swift Current Creek, already swollen from spring run-off, would rise further as the sun melted the remaining snow. Adelaide turned and saw Hughes studying the stream.

"He going to move the water. Maybe, he find gold," Alex said. They saw him shake his head.

"He don't know nothing," Adelaide laughed.

Hughes questioned Alex about other prospectors who had left Edmonton the fall before, but Alex had no idea where they might be. He was completely uninterested in gold. "Maybe they went out to the railroad," he said. "By canoe, don't take long. Slow with horses."

Hughes set beaver traps as Alex did. He would thus, Adelaide knew, have something to do while he watched for prospectors.

Over the days, no prospectors appeared, and Hughes caught nothing.

Adelaide looked at his sets. "Pretty dumb beaver if he gets caught," she concluded. "Mosie sets a better trap."

Although Adelaide dismissed Hughes, Alex was quite willingly to return his friendliness whenever it was offered.

"How come you so nice?" Adelaide asked.

Alex shrugged. "Hughes is old. Sometimes he's cranky."

One day after weeks of intermittent quarrels, Alex and Hughes travelled as far as Starvation Camp, a half day's ride.

Kid Price and Jack Evans had a cabin there, and Alex was pleased to see his old trapping partner. Two years earlier, Alex McCaulay had met Kid Price, and throughout the following winter, Alex and Kid became partners and friends trapping on the Canoe River. In the spring Alex and his family returned east to Henry House while Kid went south to Beavermouth, near Golden.

Hughes claimed Alex's friends for his own. Jack was strong and quiet. His word was backed by knowledge. Kid's lively

brown eyes drew everyone into his conversation. Kid's wiry
frame lent conviction to his tale of rugged adventure.

They spent the afternoon discussing prospecting possibili-
ties, and Hughes heard that Swift Current Creek was low
enough to set up sluice boxes only in the fall and winter. They
discussed the best routes into and out of the area, and Kid
repeated the tales he had heard of gold on the Finlay and the
Peace. Hughes' eyes glinted. He said he must go further, perhaps
to the Finlay, the Peace, or even to the Yukon.

On their way back, Alex and Hughes met two prospectors
who were on their way out, and the prospectors travelled with
them and talked of their prospecting adventures all the way.
Those prospectors camped at Swift Current Creek for the night,
then continued on to Edmonton while Hughes stayed behind.

Hughes was in top spirits. A week of peace followed.
Nothing Alex did annoyed Hughes. He wanted a guide. Alex
and his family could travel with him wherever the rivers took
them. When Alex hesitated, Hughes brushed off his objections.
He brought sugar, flour, bacon, and beans from his hoarded
supplies to share with the family. He spread syrup on the
children's bannock.

"The Fraser River will carry us to where we cut over to the
Parsnip, and gold prospects are good in the Parsnip. You heard
Kid and Jack. We can talk to them again, get some more
directions. If you get tired of it, you can go down the Parsnip
and down the Peace, and you'll be back east of the mountains,
just north of your home. Give you a chance to see some country."
All these things Hughes said to Alex.

Still, after days of Hughes' talk, Alex was adamant. He was
going home.

Hughes exploded in fury. "Give me my furs," he shouted.

"What furs?" Alex asked.

"You know damn well what furs," Hughes said. He turned
and went into his tent. Alex and Hughes did not see each other
or speak again that day.

Chapter V

Four-year-old Mosie assembled the collection of stones he hoped to add to the horse's pack while Mary, the baby, took a last taste of stones, sticks, and anything else she could put in her mouth. This elicited an occasional "Tch-tch" from her mother as she dismantled the teepee and carefully folded the canvas into a neat package.

Alex collected the horses, removed the hobbles from the old black mare, and waited while she drank from the mountain stream. It was the twelfth of June, 1899, and beaver trapping season was over. Alex and Adelaide were packing to leave their camp near Mount Robson.

Adelaide saw Hughes sullenly watching from his tent. He had quarrelled with Alex again last night and demanded furs again this morning. Seeing his shifty gaze and remembering the wihtikow, she shuddered, shaking off the foreboding. Although she still felt uncomfortable in his presence, to Adelaide, Hughes was as insignificant as the light filmy cloud clinging to the mountain whose snowy cap spiralled above the surrounding peaks—as insignificant as the horseflies that constantly annoyed. Tomorrow, she thought, he will be here, the mountains will be between us, and I'll be glad of it.

Adelaide folded the blankets neatly, formed the beaver hides into a packet and tied them with gut. She had a cooking pot, a tea pail, traps, and Alex's rifle—all their few possessions—ready beneath the teepee poles.

While she worked, Alex had saddled all the horses except for the young mare which was restive. Adelaide left Mosie to guard Mary under the still standing teepee poles while she held the halter and Alex saddled the fractious horse. He talked softly to the mare to calm her. He bent low to reach under her belly for the cinch.

Hughes stepped from his tent, raised his rifle, and aimed carefully at the stooped figure. Alex glanced up, and Hughes fired.

Adelaide jumped back. The horse whinnied and bolted. Mosie, wide eyed and watching, crouched and placed a protective hand on Mary silencing her.

Alex moaned and crumpled down. Blood streamed from his face, over his hands, his shirt, and his pants. It splattered on the ground at his feet.

Adelaide stared at his bloody face. Her eyes followed the blood as it streamed down to the ground. She saw him falter and grabbed for him.

Alex emitted a slurred *"Namoya!"* He flung out his arms striking her in the face.

She staggered back. *"Keqway? Keqway?"* she cried. She heard the rifle bolt click and whirled. Hughes had removed the spent shell, let it drop at his feet. He was reloading.

She ran to him, placed a restraining hand on his arm deflecting the gun. *"Tanehki?"* she implored.

"Away, slut!" Hughes flung Adelaide aside. He looked past her; his eyes never left Alex.

Adelaide heard Alex groan. She spun about. He slumped. She rushed to him, and keeping an eye on Hughes, she eased Alex into a more comfortable position and examined his wounds.

Hughes lowered his gun and ran to the teepee poles. The children screamed again and again.

"Our babies!" Adelaide cried. "He'll kill them!"

Alex staggered to his feet. A garbled cry, unintelligible, burst through the blood from his shattered mouth. With his hands, he pleaded. He tried to speak, staggered forward pointed to the children, rapidly shook his head, and extended his hand toward Hughes in a gesture Adelaide knew acknowledged defeat.

Hughes picked up Alex's gun and removed it from its case. Carrying both guns, Hughes, an ex-boxer, strode over, shook Alex's hand as he would the hand of a combatant in the ring, and then turned and disappeared into his tent, still carrying Alex's gun.

Adelaide's arms encircled Alex as he collapsed onto the ground. *"Nisoh kumakewin!* Help me!" Adelaide implored, but only the children were there.

Together, Alex and Adelaide staggered to the teepee poles. Adelaide helped Alex down onto the spruce boughs and covered him with a blanket. She comforted the children as she grabbed the cattail fluff she had gathered for her moon time, all the while speaking rapidly to Mosie. *"Puga keneso kamoya.* We must help him," she said. "Take basket. Get fluff, much fluff. Mary help."

All the previous summer, she and Mosie had gathered berries, fuel, and fluff. Four-year-old Mosie was her constant helper. He knew what to do. Mary could not really help, but she followed Mosie while her mother tended to Alex. Both children needed to be away from the blood.

Adelaide quickly gathered some fresh young shoots of horsetail which would, she knew, stem the blood and comfort Alex. She pried a punk from a dead poplar and, lighting it, placed it near Alex. The smoke would keep the flies away. These things would comfort him while she erected the teepee over him.

The sun was high in the sky before Adelaide was able to turn to her children. They had returned long ago, dropped the basket of fluff by her side, and were huddled at the foot of the spruce bow bed, sucking their thumbs. She gathered them into her arms and went out into the sun.

Alex's horse had returned with a rope still hanging from its halter. As she removed the halter, the horse nuzzled. Weeping, she buried her face in its mane while the children clung to her. "We must go back to Papa," she said.

In the teepee, she clasped Alex's hand, and the children snuggled by her side, Mary whimpering for the breast. Adelaide put the child to nurse, but her breast was dry. Adelaide rose, kindled a fire, made a weak Labrador tea, and coaxed the child to drink. Mosie sipped at the tea while Mary sobbed till she slept.

Adelaide heard Hughes pace back and forth. She heard him come nearer and yet nearer, then turn and walk away. He did not look into the teepee; he did not speak. Silently, he paced towards the teepee, paused. She heard the rasp of his breath. She heard him pace again, pause, turn, pace back, pause, turn again. Always she heard his step on the gravel, the pause, and the rasping breath.

She heard him leave, split wood; she smelled tea and bacon. When the children began to whimper, Adelaide gave them each a bone from the smoked beaver to gnaw. Hughes had offered them nothing to eat, offered no help. Adelaide did not know what she would do if he did. He had both guns.

She began a low mournful chant. The children clung tightly. Alex tossed and moaned. She spoke softly to them. "I must fix Papa," she said, and they huddled together.

The bullet had torn Alex's mouth, and he could not drink. She moistened the side of his mouth away from the wound, and with moss she sponged his face. His right eye was gone. The bullet had shattered his upper and lower jaw, re-entered at his chest, and lodged in his abdomen, just under the skin. She cleaned the wounds as best she could. She could do no more.

As she tried to comfort her family, she beseeched her Creator. What could she do? She couldn't move Alex. What would Hughes do? Why did he stay? He had Alex's gun while she had only her knife. She took it up and hid it in her dress. She would keep it with her always.

The children, exhausted, fell asleep early, but soon awakened screaming. Adelaide comforted them as best she could. Her breasts had dried completely, so there was no comfort there for Mary. She patted them and rocked them, and finally, they slept again. Alex groaned the whole night. Even as he slept he moaned. At sun-up, she would seek herbs.

Chapter VI

The children awoke, and whimpering, they shook Adelaide free from her trance. They were hungry and cold. The temperature had dropped; frost coated the ground, and a chill seeped through the teepee.

Adelaide wrapped both children in her warm blanket and then, creeping out through the morning chill, she gathered lichen and dry twigs and lit them. She split some larger branches which she carefully laid over the flames. A pole braced over the fire pit held the tea pail which she filled at the creek, she picked and added a few leaves of Labrador tea. Then, she made bannock from the meagre supply of flour, and carried it in to the children.

Alex was still unable to eat, and as she sponged his dry lips, she shuddered at the odor of Hughes' grouse stew wafting on the air. "Today it is grouse," she thought, "but a wihtikow eats man."

She forced her mind back to feeding her children. Alex had cached flour for the return trip, but it was two day's travel away. Indian potato grew on the slide, lilies grew along the river, but she could not leave Alex to go for them; nor could she leave Alex while she fished. Hughes had Alex's gun.

She would set snares for game. In the meantime, the children would eat the bannock, and she would eat the beaver she had dried. She could grab a few willow herbs when she went for water.

On the morning of the third day, after a fitful sleep, Adelaide woke. She must have help. She couldn't go for food;

soon the flour would be gone, and the children would starve. Alex's wounds were infected, and she couldn't keep the flies away from them. She neglected Mary who whimpered the whole day. Mosie followed Adelaide mutely.

Ask Hughes, Alex gestured. When she shuddered, Alex said, "Namoya!" Hughes isn't a wihtikow, he gestured. He crossed himself and touched the cross at his neck. Alex was angry. Hughes is a bad man, not a wihtikow, he gestured. You dreamed, he gestured. Adelaide's shrug ended in a shudder. Alex had said all this before.

"Still," she thought, "if I don't get help, Alex will die. A bad man, Hughes is, but good or bad, he is the only one here. He took the saddles off the horses," she reasoned. "Maybe, he is not angry with Alex today. Some days he is friends with Alex. Maybe Alex will promise to take him to the Yukon. Maybe, he will let Alex live for a few days. Maybe, someone will come before Hughes changes into a wihtikow."

Chapter VII

A delaide shuddered as she asked Hughes for help. He came. He carried water, and he brought wood. That night he sat with Alex while Adelaide tried to sleep.

The smell of rotting blood, of infected wounds crept into Adelaide's nostrils. Death hovered. She dozed and woke in a cold sweat. The wihtikow slunk into the teepee. She looked again, only Hughes was there. She laid shivering till dawn.

Had she dozed? When she looked about, Hughes was gone. Alex lay in a trance, a kind of sleep, his jaw ragged and red. Adelaide saw that the wihtikow had nibbled at it, at his jaw and at his neck.

When the children wakened whimpering, they found Adelaide rocking back and forth in a mournful chant. They shook her repeatedly, and she finally woke to them. She pulled them to her and hugged them tightly. She must care for them and protect them because their papa could not. She built a fire and made bannock for them. Death's odor stole her appetite, but the children scrambled for every crumb, then sucked on dried beaver meat.

Hughes returned with food to cook over her fire. As the bacon and beans cooked, Adelaide saw the look of expectation on Mosie's and Mary's faces, and she quaked in fear.

Adelaide watched as Hughes speared the bacon and poured beans into a tin plate. He chewed the bacon, took great mouthfuls of beans, and slurped down the hot boiled tea. He offered them nothing. The children clung to their mother and whimpered, and she clutched them to her in chagrin and relief.

Hughes had not fed them. He had not started to draw them into the wihtikow's power.

"Damned crying bloody brats," Hughes cursed as he gathered the last of his breakfast and stomped back to his tent.

Adelaide would not ask for his help again. Alex no longer wanted it.

"Why can't Hughes go where the children wouldn't see? Then, I could kill him. When my man dies, I will take my knife, and I will kill Hughes. Then I will take my children from here." Bitterly, hopelessly, Adelaide wept silently.

Another day followed. Adelaide stopped the bleeding, but Alex continued to suffer. Both his upper and lower jaw, broken, clenched involuntarily. He clutched his face and moaned. Although he was choking with thirst, he could not drink. He no longer showed interest in food. The flies would not leave him alone. Blow flies crawled over him, and black flies bit him incessantly. The broken ribs made breathing difficult, and inflammation had spread to the chest wound. With his fingers, he worried at the bullet in his abdomen.

Adelaide did what she could each day. She gathered a few herbs, lit a small fire, made bannock, and fed the children. She brought water, and then she returned to Alex's side. She bathed his face and wet his lips and placed herbs on his wounds. Hunger gnawed at her. Sometimes Alex rose and pointed towards Hughes' tent. He made stabbing motions, then fell back on the bed.

She continued her chant. Soon, she thought, the wihtikow will take him. He will be gone from me.

She set a snare for rabbits, and Mosie sneaked from the teepee through the bushes to check the snare. A wolverine had eaten the rabbit. Mosie brought a bit of rabbit fur. They remembered rabbit meat, and they cried.

Chapter VIII

On the fifth day, when Mosie was checking the snare, Adelaide poked her head out to check on him. She inhaled the breeze, and its spirit spoke to her. It brought the scent of tobacco, the murmur of voices, the tramping of horses.

A horse whinnied. Mosie came running.

"People coming," he said. "Horses coming. I hear them. Our horses hear them."

Adelaide motioned Mosie quiet. She beckoned him into the teepee. The spirit had not spoken to Hughes. She patted Mosie's head and touched her lips. She pointed to Mary. While she crept out to check, she knew, Mosie and Mary would stay with their papa, and they would be very quiet.

Men across the stream. Camping. Five, maybe six. One looked up. She waved frantically. He spoke, but the water carried his voice away. She waved again, and he swam his horse across.

"*Paskshot!*" she wept. "*Ni napim paskshow ow!*"

He turned and called, "Come over here, Dan. There seems to be trouble. I can't talk Indian."

The water carried his voice away.

Chapter IX

Dan Noyes Jr., was a small fair complexioned man with beady eyes. Except for an accent, nothing betrayed his Métis origins. The Cree accent sounded strange on his lips.

As Dan and his companions approached the camp, Hughes came walking toward them. Dan's companions greeted Hughes.

"What happened?" one man asked.

"I shot the boy," Hughes answered. "You'd better go see him."

Dan turned from them and ran to the teepee. He knelt by the injured man.

"Alex!" he cried. " My god, Alex!"

"Dan!" Tears streamed from Alex's good eye.

"What happened, Alex? What happened?" Dan clutched Alex's hand. He examined the gaping hole that had been Alex's eye, the torn jaw, the distorted face.

Alex freed his hand and pointed to Hughes' tent. He pointed toward the pelts. "*Muqway*," he said. "Nothing! For two beaver skins," he signed. "For nothing I will die." Alex clutched Dan's shirt. He rose and made the motion of pointing a rifle at Hughes' tent. Shoot him, Dan, Alex gestured and fell back. His eyes pleaded.

"Namoya! Namoya," Dan answered. "No! No! I dare not. The Mounties will take care of him. I'll stay with you, I promise. Jack Evans and Kid Price are at Starvation Flats. One of the others 'll go for them."

Listening, Adelaide whispered, "*Manitou!*" Memories filled her, memories of that cold winter's night on the Canoe

River: smell of balsam, steam rising, a cocoon of blankets, of furs, Mosie—coughing, choking, a yellow plaster on Mosie's chest, a winter night, cold, so cold out, fire burning in the hearth, the cabin warm, Kid working methodically, rubbing Mosie's arms and legs, changing wet clothes for dry, using Alex's or his old shirt, underwear, anything in the cabin.

She remembered how gentle Kid was with Mosie, how much like family. Alex had explained, "Kid's mama had many babies. He remembers his brothers and his sisters."

"*Nistow!*" she breathed. "Kid will look after Alex. He will look after us."

When the prospectors entered the teepee, Dan spoke to them in Cree. Realizing his mistake, he burst out, "I tried to make little jokes with him. I wanted to make him feel better, but he told me he is going to die."

The plans of the prospectors on their way to Edmonton came to a sudden stop. They felt helpless in the face of Alex's massive wounds; they were shocked, too, at the mess Hughes' ridiculous temper had created. Joseph Hostyn and Henry Hollings followed Dan's suggestion and went for Kid. If Kid could tend to the trapper, as Dan assured them he could, they would continue their interrupted trip to Edmonton.

Chapter X

" Jack and I were working in our garden when Joe and Henry arrived after the shooting. I was hoeing the potatoes," Percy said.

Clara was at the hotel taking her afternoon nap. Percy had made coffee and added a shot of rum. He sat leaning on his elbows at the table while Alan had sunk his bulk comfortably into the easy chair. They were discussing the shooting.

"I ditched that hoe, and we saddled our horses as quick as we could. Joe and Henry didn't seem to know their friends might be in danger, but my god! When a man starts shooting, who knows what might happen? Let me tell you, we rode at a goodly clip.

"When we got there, Hughes greeted us as if there was just a bit of a mess for me to clean up. 'He's in the tent with his woman and Dan,' Hughes said. I wheeled away from Hughes and rushed to the teepee."

"Six days in a teepee in the summer's heat; no disinfectant and no way to clean the wounds. The family must have been in a state," the doctor interposed.

"Mosie ran to meet me and clung to me as if he was pursued by all the devils of hell," Percy continued. "Adelaide stood with Mary clinging to her, and the tears streamed from both pairs of eyes. I knelt beside Alex and took his hand. He clung to me.

"The wounds were crawling with maggots. A blow fly, drunk from blood, crawled away from Alex's neck. I started to question Alex, and he placed his hand over his heart and shook his head.

"Dan spoke up. 'He can't speak English because of the wound in his jaw,' Dan said. 'you'll have to read his gestures. He speaks a little Cree—the words that are spoken in the throat. You know. Ehe is yes. Namoya, no, is indistinct. God! I'm glad to see you!'

"I began to examine the wounds. 'Pain?' I asked, and 'Mmm!' Alex nodded. 'And here?' 'Mmm!'

"The Indians burn that fungus that grows on poplar. It smoulders, and the smoke drives the flies away. I sent Dan to find more of it. The flies would swarm all around the place at sun up.

"You wouldn't believe Hughes' gall. When Dan left the teepee, Hughes entered with Joe, and knelt down beside me as cozy as could be. Joe started to introduce him.

" 'I've met him,' I said. I rose to my feet and turned on Hughes. 'I suppose you are the person responsible for this.'

" 'Yes. I shot him,' Hughes admitted just like that.

" 'You did a hell of a bad job!' I told him, and Hughes just looked at me hesitantly as if he couldn't believe what he was hearing, and then he turned and left the tent, and Joe followed. They didn't come back."

"Did the man have no conscience?" Dr. Keller asked appalled.

"Alex was only an Indian," Percy said sardonically.

"I've worked in some primitive conditions," the doctor said. "But at least I had a kitchen table to operate on. I had white linen, disinfectants, something to kill the pain, and there were screens to keep the flies away. But in a teepee? Whew! What did you do?"

"I'd been in the back country for over twenty years and seen a few accidents, you know. I'd learned to be prepared for emergencies. I had medical supplies at our winter camp three miles up the creek. Jack went for them.

"I had morphine and laudanum, carbolic acid, permanganate of potash, some bandages, salves, flax seed, hypodermic syringes, needles, dentists forceps, that sort of thing," Percy explained.

The doctor scratched his head. "And where did you get all that, and how did you know what to get?"

"I'd talked to doctors in my travels. The stuff was easy enough to get. But as for linen, we didn't have so much as a linen handkerchief among the lot of us that was fit to use. Adelaide had a Hudson Bay blanket, some moosehides, and a bear skin. The smell of blood on them was sickening, but I couldn't do much more then rinse the blood off. Even summer nights are cold in the mountains, and we needed those blankets. I had to augment the bandages with moss and the fluff that Adelaide was using. There is something to be said for the Indian remedies. In time I learned about them. Percy stretched and yawned. "You know, Alan, you'll have to excuse me," he said. "Clara isn't the only one who needs a wee nap."

"Yes!" the doctor replied. "Well, you go ahead. I'll just lean back in this chair."

When Hughes left the teepee, Adelaide closed the flap over the entrance. Later when she stepped out into the air, she saw Hughes and Joe crossing the stream to the Edmonton men's camp. Hughes was carrying a bottle of rum.

While Kid tended to Alex, Jack had gone with the prospectors for dinner. Hughes laced their coffee generously with rum. When the men began to talk of Alex's condition, Hughes said little. He looked sullenly off into space.

"I can't see what your friend can do for that poor breed," said one man. "I don't know why he's still alive. He's a hell of a mess."

"Kid'll do all he can." Jack said.

"Christ! His face is half shot off, and I don't know what that bullet did to his chest," said another.

Jack shook his head. "Yes! He is in bad shape."

After dinner, Jack excused himself. He went to the teepee, checked on Kid and he left on foot, because it was dark, for their winter camp up the creek. He was afraid to trust a horse's footing on the steep mountain trail in the dark.

Throughout the three mile trip, he depended on the light of the moon to pick out familiar landmarks. The trail was well marked where horses' hooves had cut into the sandy shore, but as it followed the stream past towering cliffs and over flat rock surfaces, it became indistinct, and Jack had to rely on his knowledge of the area to carry him to his destination.

Once there, Jack quickly retrieved the necessary medical supplies and hurried back down stream over the rocks carrying the treasures with him.

Meanwhile at the teepee, Adelaide hovered beside Kid as he worked over Alex. She must see; see what he could do for Alex.

In spite of Adelaide's efforts to keep a smudge, the wounds were alive with maggots. Kid boiled water then cooled it and swabbed out the mess. He tried to pick out the crawling putrid mass.

Alex fainted.

Kid worked over Alex. He put a cold damp cloth to the sides of his head and called to him insistently. When Alex revived, Kid sent Dan to the prospector's camp for a funnel. He attempted to pour water into Alex, but, at the first spoonful of water, Alex gagged.

Adelaide pushed forward, and held him. While the water drained from his mouth, her tears streamed down.

"I'm sorry," Kid said as he moved in again and washed Alex. "I'll be careful." He massaged Alex's arms and back, trying to give him some degree of comfort.

"Thank God!" Kid said when a returning Jack Evans handed him the medical supplies. "Thank God!" He quickly prepared a needle and injected Alex with morphine.

Alex sighed and relaxed, and Adelaide suddenly slumped. As if the medicine had been given to her, she curled close to her children, and in a moment, she slept.

Kid prepared a carbolic disinfectant, and syringed out the wounds. He made a poultice of flax seed, and covered the infected areas. By candlelight, he could do no more.

Jack stayed in the teepee while Kid provided what relief he could to the suffering man. Then because Dan had chosen to stay near Alex and would be there to help, Jack went back to the prospectors' camp. Dan with his quick perception would forestall any danger from Hughes at the teepee, while Jack could do the same at the other camp.

Chapter XI

The next morning as daylight filtered into the teepee, Kid looked at his surroundings. Alex slept on a bed of spruce boughs and a caribou hide. His coat and a single blanket were thrown over him. The children, curled together for warmth, slept on boughs and were covered with a blanket of rabbit fur. Adelaide's arm lay across them.

Beaver pelts were bundled ready to go; a tea pail hung from one of the poles; a frying pan, tin cups and plates, a ladle fashioned from a tin can, were stacked together; a tinned kettle hung from another pole; a jam tin held a few cupfuls of flour; some dried beaver meat hung from another pole.

The only food was dried beaver and a couple of cups of flour!

Jack came over from the prospector's tent. His stocky figure, blue eyes, auburn beard and mustache exuded calmness. "Hughes is over breakfasting with his friends," he said. "A good time to look for guns."

Together, they went into the tent. Two rifles! Right in his bed! Not loaded. Shells right there, where he could grab them . . . even in the dark.

They checked around. Food was plentiful: flour, sugar, tea, bacon, beans, prunes, raisins, and tinned jam. At least three months supply of grub! They looked at each other and shook their heads, then turned to go. Jack Evans took the shells and both guns. As he disappeared with the guns, Kid returned to the teepee.

Adelaide had lit a fire beside the teepee and was making bannock for the children. Mosie ran and clung to Kid's hand, and Kid stopped to talk with Adelaide.

"You help Alex?" Adelaide asked.

"I try my very best," Kid answered.

"Manitou help," Adelaide said. "You help!" She nodded, and Kid sighed.

Alex lay awake twitching restlessly.

"Any better?" Kid asked.

So, so, Alex gestured.

When Kid removed the poultices, Alex placed Kid's hand over the wound on his abdomen. He mumbled indistinctly, but Kid could not understand the Cree. Alex winced and gestured. It hurts, his gestures said. He drew his hand across the swelling in a cutting motion, then placed his thumb over the bullet and flipped his hand away in an outward motion. Remove it, his gesture said.

Kid nodded, but his attempt to locate the bullet failed. "Sorry! Can't take it out today," he said. "Maybe when the swelling goes down." He administered a laudanum sedative.

He swabbed the putrid sores, and picked out more maggots, then poulticed the sores again, including the area over the bullet. He could do nothing with the wound in the chest except to poultice the bullet hole.

"What will we do with that bastard?" Kid asked Jack.

"I'll talk to the men. Someone will help me take him to Golden," Jack assured him. "But first, I'll go to our winter camp and get some grub."

"Yeah," Kid said. "I'm not anxious to eat with Hughes and his friends; Adelaide and the babies are starved. Dan and I'll be here, too, for a while yet. You can get what you need for the trip from the cabin at Starvation Flats."

"Bannock?" Adelaide offered as they emerged. There was so little.

Jack rubbed his stomach and shook his head. He was full. Kid accepted a tiny portion. The bannock was made from the last of her flour; they wouldn't eat again until Jack returned.

Chapter XII

Now that Kid stayed in the teepee, Adelaide was free to leave the sick-bed for the first time in days. She and the children wandered about the campsite relaxing in the pleasant weather. They came to the foot of the trail and followed it up stream. Mary insisted on walking, but much of the time Adelaide stooped and lifted her from rock to rock. Suddenly, Mary buried her face in the tiny twinflowers, then in the moss. She traced the lichen on the rocks with her finger. Mosie ran ahead and back. He touched everything; he picked up pebbles, bugs and sticks. They climbed over huge boulders, and saw water spreading over a large table-like rock and tumbling below. Mary stood, imitated the sound, laughed, and Mosie copied her. Soon they had made a song of the brook, interspersed with children's laughter.

Adelaide watched her children as they absorbed their surroundings. She saw their happy release and thought of them, babies, imprisoned in the teepee. For days they had watched; they had listened to their papa suffer. She dreaded taking them back, but now, she had to return to Alex.

"Come!" She said. "We should go to papa."

They clambered down over the rocks again till they reached a spot near the crossing where the stream settled into a quiet pool. Screened from view by soopolallie bushes, they stopped to listen to the murmur of the water and peer about. If they were silent, birds would come near. Maybe even rabbits, or mink. Fish would rest in the shaded water.

Adelaide sniffed the air. Tobacco! She motioned to Mosie who sniffed and nodded. They heard voices, and crouched down. Adelaide placed a quieting hand on Mary.

"Evans says I should go out to the railroad and turn myself in," Hughes said.

"Suit yourself." Bill Cook, who had, formerly, been Hughes partner, answered coldly. "The Moberlys will be in here soon. You'll be food for the ravens if you stick around."

"Well, Christ! He was robbing me. What else could I do? I got mad and I shot."

"Well, he has friends, and you're in trouble. You should have had better sense." Bill's voice exuded disgust.

"We'll stick by you. That's a sure thing. We can't let the buggers get away with that," Hollings pronounced.

Bill looked at Hollings contemptuously.

"Well the plan is, Evans goes out with me, and Price stays with the buck and his squaw," Hughes continued. "I bet Price will like that, eh—some tender smoked meat."

"Yeah Hughes, I've been wondering. Was it beaver pelts you fought over or maybe smoked meat?" Hollings questioned with a laugh.

"Hell! I coulda had that any time—a bottle of rum to Alex."

"Keep your mouth shut, you fool!" Bill exploded. If Dan or Kid hear you, you're dead today."

As the men stepped out onto the log to cross the water, their voices faded.

"They talked about papa," Mosie whispered. "Hughes said, 'I shot.'"

"Ehe," Adelaide sighed. "They talked about papa." Adelaide understood some of what they said.

She pulled her children to her, folded them in her arms, and sobbed. The tears streamed down onto the children, and they clung to her.

After a time, Mosie stirred. "We should go to Papa," he said.

When Adelaide rose, she was as anxious as Mosie to return to Alex. While Mosie tugged and Mary clung to her neck,

Adelaide rushed along. She entered the teepee, set Mary down, and knelt beside Alex. The children tentatively reached out and touched him. Alex rested his hand over theirs.

Mosie stayed for a few moments, then slipped away silently. He crept out and sat by the entrance and watched.

Chapter XIII

When Jack left with Hughes and the prospectors, Dan, Kid, Adelaide, Mosie, and Mary stayed with the dying Alex. Bill Cook and the other prospector went up the creek to the claims they had filed the year before. Although the water was too high for them to work the claim, they could build a cabin for later in the year, and they were nearby, within call.

Kid returned to his patient and removed the poultices. The swelling on the abdomen had decreased so that he could feel the bullet under the skin. He administered morphine.

Adelaide watched as Alex crossed himself, and Dan told the beads and said the prayers they had learned at the mission. Adelaide beseeched Manitou. She did not know which god would send help, if any. Kid's medicine took the pain away.

Alex fell into a deep sleep, and Adelaide noted how peaceful he looked.

"Take the children out," Kid said. He let Adelaide feel the bullet just under the skin. A very small cut, he gestured. Alex will be O.K., he gestured, and Dan explained in Cree.

Adelaide took Mosie and Mary by the hand, and they walked out along the stream. The children picked flowers for their papa. Pinto came and nuzzled Adelaide's hand. She petted him and placed the children on his back. They stopped, chattered back to the squirrels, and invited them to come see papa.

Adelaide buried her face in the horse's mane and hugged her children. Surely Alex will live, she thought. All the spirits are with him. He must live. She begged Pinto's spirit for help.

Kid came and walked with Adelaide and the children back to the teepee. As they knelt down, Adelaide reached out and touched Alex's cheek. He opened his eyes.

"We've brought Pinto to see you," Mosie piped, and Mary, who had been fearful of Alex's battered face, now attempted to crawl into his arms. Adelaide pulled them back, and Alex smiled and slept again. Adelaide sat silently at his side. The children curled together at her feet.

Each day Alex became weaker. The infection in the chest wound developed into pleurisy, and Kid made a steam from Friar's Balsam. He applied a mustard plaster, avoiding the open wound. Alex moaned and pulled it off. Kid increased the morphine.

Nothing of the ministrations by Adelaide or Kid, no pleas to the spirits, or Dan's prayers to the Christian God, could help Alex. On the night of the twenty-fourth of June, 1899, Alex McCaulay died in the presence of his wife, his two children, and his friends, Dan Noyes and Kid Price. Prospectors came from their camp nearby. Kid had a small bottle of rum, and together, they held a wake for Alex far into the night.

Another afternoon, another evening, another night, and two more days had passed. Percy had guided his visitors on a tour of the sights in downtown Victoria. They visited the harbour, the Empress Hotel, the Legislature, Chinatown, and Beacon Hill Park. The weather had changed during the night, and on the morning of the third day, they woke to a dismal light; the wind spattered a steady drizzle against the glass.

They decided it was not a day for sight-seeing, and instead, Clara and Alan visited with Percy at the residence. They settled in the lounge and the cook sent sugar cookies and tea.

"Isn't this lovely!" Clara said. "So thoughtful! How did you find this place?"

"Actually, the doctor found it for me. I had a bit of pneumonia," Percy began. "I was a month in the hospital, and the doctor thought I should have someone to look after me for a while.

"I'm better now. I planned to go home and was waiting to hear from a partner to go prospecting with me. Then, I got your letter, and I waited for your visit. I've really enjoyed staying here. The roof doesn't leak, I'm always warm, and I don't have to bare my behind in that cold outhouse in the winter. I'm afraid I'm getting soft."

The doctor smiled at this comment and then turned the conversation to Alex's death. Percy's guests sat for two hours, mesmerized as he recounted those painful days nearly sixty years past.

"There wasn't another thing you could have done," Dr. Keller said when Percy concluded. "Infection had a week to develop before you saw him. Even in a hospital with trained staff, before miracle drugs I lost patients with lesser injuries. Not many people were as hardy as Mama and you. Not many survived everything to live a long life. You removed the bullet and gave him peace of mind. That was good."

"That's not what the lawyer said," Percy responded. "By the time he got through with me, I thought I was on my way to the gallows."

"Well, that's a lawyer's job," the doctor said, "lawyers aren't paid to be nice, are they?"

"The poor woman! The poor children! How terrible it must have been for them," Clara cried. "I hope you could give Alex a Christian burial, at least."

"We did indeed, my dear Clara. I'm very much ashamed to say we didn't consider Adelaide's preference," Percy responded. "That funeral was no comfort to her."

Clara reached over and slapped Percy's hand. "Oh! Percy! You are the limit. Alex was a Christian and deserved a Christian burial."

"You've been sitting for hours," Percy laughed. "It's time I made a spot of tea. I wish you had met Adelaide," he added thoughtfully. "She was nearer your age than mine. Nobody with feeling could help but love her just as she was."

Chapter XIV

L ater that night while her children slept, Adelaide lay awake and recalled each moment of her life with Alex.

Her family was camped on the shore of Brule Lake. As she played with her younger brothers and sisters, she saw from a great distance, the rider and stallion, black hair, black mane and tale, streaming in the wind. Up and down they floated on the air, and as they neared, she saw neither saddle nor bridle but only a narrow leather rein from hand to horse. He reined in. He talked to her. To her alone. His black eyes told her she was woman.

Their life together had been good. Alex was a warm-hearted lover. Always he said she was the prettiest, the only one. When she tended her babies, Alex came, and when the child was fed, she handed it to Alex, and he danced with the baby in his arms. Alex was affectionate with the children and thoughtful of her. Some of her cousins were not so fortunate.

Even of her resentment of Hughes, she thought, "I didn't want him to come between us. I didn't think he was evil, no more than Alex did. Alex never knew thirty summers, and I, scarcely twenty. Our life is over."

Adelaide wept.

She remembered the grave that Hughes had dug, the grave that filled with water. Dan had taken a shovel and filled in the useless pit. Adelaide chanted a mournful prayer that continued all through the night, a plea to Manitou.

Early on the day of the funeral, Kid and Dan located a dry spot on a knoll. They looked down on the stream, up to the mountain. They consulted with Adelaide. She walked around with the children, looked up to the mountain, down to the stream, around at the shrubs and lichen. "Yes," she said, "This is the place."

Dan and Kid began to dig. Bill Cook, hearing the shovel scrape the rocks, came to spell them off. Soon they had a grave. From a dry spruce, Dan Noyes and Kid Price had split planks and made a coffin. They carried the coffin to the grave site.

When all were assembled, Dan conducted prayers in Latin. In the mission, he had listened to the priest and he had memorized the words: powerful words to a powerful God. He didn't know their meaning, but God did.

In her mind, Adelaide chanted, silently chanted her own prayer, a silent prayer to Manitou. Dan picked up a handful of earth and dropped it on the coffin, and all those assembled did the same. Dan placed a cross at the head of the grave on which Kid had carved, 'Alex McCaulay, Shot June 12, 1899, Died June 24, 1899.' As Dan escorted Adelaide and the children away, Kid and the prospectors took shovels and covered the coffin.

Adelaide wanted a small house constructed over the grave, a house for Alex's spirit. She would leave the teepee for Alex's spirit. When his spirit wandered from the grave it would have another home in the teepee. Adelaide wanted that house built so Alex's spirit wouldn't wander too far, but she was silent.

Among these white men, she was silent. She would build it. But Dan knew. Although he and Alex had learned from the priests, Dan knew that the whiteman's ritual did not comfort Adelaide.

"Alex's spirit needs a house," he said.

Kid brought hammer, nails, and a saw from his winter cabin. He shaped a ridge pole and supports. He split shakes and Dan nailed them to the ridge pole; a shelter over the grave. Kid built a fence to mark and protect the spot.

Chapter XV

In the morning, before Kid and Dan woke, Adelaide took feathers, porcupine quills, beads and sinew and fashioned a charm which she hung by Alex's grave. She gathered her horses and tethered them behind the teepee. Mosie and Mary sat, watched, and munched on bannock while Adelaide worked quietly and methodically. She would leave the teepee for Alex's spirit. If his spirit roamed from the grave, it would find the teepee for a home. She would leave a blanket, a tea pail, a little food. The rest she packed.

"Home now!" She answered Kid's query.

"No! No! Namoya!" Kid said. "You come with us," he gestured.

Adelaide carefully folded the blankets and hides.

Kid sputtered. "Tell her Dan. Tell her. She's the only witness. She must come to Golden. She must!"

Dan began to explain. "You must tell the Redcoats. They come and get you. They should know how Alex died. You tell them what the old man did. Only you saw. I promised Alex the Redcoats would get Hughes. Alex's spirit must rest. A few days, then you go home. I talk for you. I take you home."

Adelaide shrugged. She was so tired. Alex's spirit must rest. If she started home now, she had almost no food for the children. If she went with Kid and Dan her children could eat. She could go home after.

Adelaide accepted the change of plan, and methodically packed utensils, supplies, and her furs. Those of her possessions that she would not need, she cached. She would retrieve them on her return. Kid had his tent and camping equipment. A canvas fly would do for overnight camping on the way.

Dan readied the pack horses while the children followed Kid as he caught and saddled his own, Mosie's, and Adelaide's horses. The children were willing enough to go with Kid.

When all was ready, Kid seated Mosie on Pinto and instructed the boy to follow close behind him. Mosie absorbed his every word and nodded solemnly. Mary, delighted to be chosen, rode with Kid. Adelaide followed Mosie, and behind her, Dan held a pack horse on a lead rope. The other horses followed. Bill Cook would accompany the party. He knew help would be needed crossing the swamps and the flooding streams.

"It's little enough for me to do," he said.

Adelaide sat dully, as dull as the leaden sky. She paid no attention to her surroundings but gave her horse its head; it could follow or not as it chose. When Dan rode up beside her and began to wheedle, to try to convince her of the necessity of the trip, she turned away.

"Watch the pack horses," she said. "I am going. Isn't that enough?"

Dan and Bill were having difficulty with the three strings of horses. McCaulay's and Cook's horses, on a trail that lead further from home, followed reluctantly. Kid's horses, which were heading home, travelled willingly, too willingly; it was difficult to keep all the horses together. Dan led one of Adelaide's reluctant string and the rest followed. Adelaide's last horse kicked out viciously at Cook's horse whenever it neared, and Cook, with much effort, kept his horses in line.

They followed the Fraser River for several hours before they came to the ford. On that cloudy day, although the river was high, it was not dangerously so. The melt from the mountains and glaciers was minimal. Nonetheless, Adelaide strapped Mary firmly to her back. Mosie dismounted, climbed on behind Kid, and clung tightly. Dan clasped the rope from Adelaide's horse, moved up stream, and they plunged in. Kid followed with his horses.

Once across, Dan returned to help with the other horses. Dan led Adelaide's lead pack horse up stream above the ford and plunged into the river with a string of horses behind. Bill Cook followed with his string, while Kid, on the far shore, prepared to rescue any animal that lost its footing.

After they crossed, Kid proposed a rest. Adelaide had already dismounted, and loosening the bands holding Mary, tied her horse to a tree. The children, hesitantly, sought their mother. Adelaide took them by the hand and walked away. If the men want tea, she thought, they will do the woman's work.

Wild strawberries peeked out among the grass along the river. Adelaide knelt down, and together she and the children picked, and the children ate. Around her, wild roses bloomed; their perfume scented the soft breeze. Gradually, the aroma seeped into her consciousness, and as she looked around, she saw them everywhere along the river bank, beside the trail. Red paint brush interspersed with yellow buttercup and white bedstraw swayed beside the stream. She walked further with the children, and they saw masses of tiny spotted orchids, of yellow moccasin flowers, of white and green lilies. A kingfisher perched on a willow branch intently watched the stream. A chickadee called cheerily. Momentarily, the sun found a break in the cloud.

Adelaide and Alex had travelled this way, but not in the early summer. Alex should be here. She gathered her children into her arms and quietly wept. Both children clung to her mutely.

When she returned to the camp, she found the men had made bannock and boiled tea. Although they didn't usually stop and build a camp fire at mid-day, the tea and the bannock smelled good. She and the children ate hungrily. Mary looked at her mother with wide eyes, and tentatively tried a chuckle. Adelaide smiled wanly and caressed her cheek.

They doused the fire and continued on, riding for several hours. Gradually the forest changed from mixed growth to pine; thin and straggly. A few sparse shrubs clung to the shifting sand, and lichen of many varieties fed on the trees and shrubs.

They rode through this primeval forest till they came to a tiny stream with a few willows along its bank; a small oasis. A cabin snuggled there. The stream emptied into a bog surrounded with grass sufficient to pasture horses. They had reached Starvation Camp, and there they stopped.

Kid augmented the supplies for their trip. Because he would buy supplies in Golden before returning to Starvation Flats, he made a list of his needs. Then he bundled his winter's catch of furs.

He held up a caribou hide. "Moccasins?" He questioned.

"Maybe. Sometime." Adelaide turned away.

The next day dawned clear and promised to be hot. They started early in order to cross the next large creek before the melt from the mountain swelled it. Their travel gradually took them away from the dry desert into larger pine with kinnikinnik, blueberry, and cranberry plants at their roots, myriad small shrubs and flowers dotting the ground.

They followed this trail along through the jackpine flats, between the eastern slopes and the McLennan River, fording each small stream as they came to it and towards mid-day came to a raging torrent with the name of Swift Creek, a name that travellers sometimes confused with Swift Current Creek.

The men separated the pack horses. Although Kid's horses forded willingly enough, the rest of the horses balked and stumbled through the rocky stream bed. Some tripped among the boulders, and the men rode into the stream to guide the pack horses to the shore and up the bank.

Adelaide and the children rode ahead until they came to the lake that spanned the valley. Here, Adelaide and Mosie dismounted and tethered their horses to trees. She left the horses behind for the men to handle, and she and the children picked their way around the swampy area between the lake and the base of the mountain. Sometimes they jumped from mossy hump to mossy hump; othertimes, they scrambled up the rocks. Once beyond the swamp, Adelaide wandered around aimlessly, waiting. She knew she should help, but she made no effort.

When Kid arrived with the horses, she and the children mounted and rode on. Their destination was The Licks, an area where fire had created good pasture. The children, already wet from fording the river, were wetter still after the swamp. They were tired, and cranky. Adelaide let the men worry the rest of the horses along.

Kid's horses had struggled through, sinking to their knees and lunging ahead. After them, the men urged the other horses as they spread out through the trees looking for better footing. Dan led McCaulay's lead horse, jerking and pulling, as it baulked and sunk in the mud. McCaulay's string followed, and Bill came behind urging them on and leading a horse of his own. Once through the swamp, they mounted again and were on their way.

Adelaide, ahead, entered onto another pine flat where she could hear the song of redwing blackbird and could see the lake below. She diverted the children by discussing the birds. Geese, ducks, loons, all the water birds nested there. Whether they saw them or not, the children were sure they had.

"Will we camp by the lake tonight?" Mosie asked.

Mosie knew the names for all. Bald eagle, redtail hawk, and raven soared above. The song of chickadee, robin, thrush, kinglet, and sparrow greeted the travellers. Jays, crows, and squirrels scolded. Caribou turned their heads from grazing and watched them pass.

When the trail forked, they took the south branch and were on the 'Tête Jaune to Golden' trail. They left the pine forest and entered mixed growth. It was cooler, wetter, and the aroma of twinflowers, wild lilies, and orchids, permeated the air. Along the banks of streams and in other open areas, wild rose bloomed in profusion. Tiny green fruit on the saskatoon and pin cherry held promise of an abundant harvest.

Adelaide absorbed her surroundings as they rode along. Alex had never been here in summer, but he had trapped here, and she could feel his spirit join her—Alex—close to her—Alex before the suffering; before the deadly shot.

A short distance down the Canoe River, they camped in pasture lush with spring growth. Horses had stumbled and had to swim while crossing Swift Creek early in the day. Much of the gear, bedding, clothing, was soaked and had to be steamed throughout the afternoon. The men hung it all to dry; they erected canvas tarps and collected firewood. They would spend the night under these tarps feeding small fires for comfort throughout a chilly night.

The next morning early, they left again because they must ford the Packsaddle before the water rose with the heat of the day. They had two more streams to cross before they reached Yellowjacket Creek and even with an early start they had little hope of arriving dry.

They left behind the wide jackpine flat, and as the river meandered through the valley, the trail sometimes followed close to the bank or sometimes left the river and plunged into a forest of huge fir and spruce. When they broke into the sun again, the path had rejoined the river. Alder flanked the path, and at times they had to fight their way through it. Deer trails branched off and disappeared.

As Adelaide rode through the timber, she saw the shadow of Alex move behind a graceful maple. Alex's spirit skirted the path throughout the day, and when they approached the cabin by Yellowjacket Creek, a cabin where they had once stayed, he stood in the doorway. Faintly, very faintly, the breeze carried Alex's voice, carried it singing a song he had learned from his father.

"And I will come again my love,
Though it were a thousand mile,"

Adelaide jumped from her horse and ran to him. Alex evaporated at her touch. She opened the cabin door, and Alex sat on the bench by the table. His black hair shone in the light from the open door and his black eyes smiled.

Her arms closed on nothing.

Adelaide sat and, rocking back and forth, she chanted, softly chanted.

Kid opened the door, saw her, and backing out, he closed the door. They would stop here. While Dan unpacked the horses, put them to pasture, and hung wet bedding to dry and Kid took the children with him.

"Come on you fellas," he said. "Let's get ourselves a fire."

Kid chopped a dry willow, and the children packed it to the fire pit. Mosie collected the two grouse that had been tied to Kid's saddle, and Kid skinned them and proceeded to make a stew.

"Astum," said Kid when he entered the cabin. "Come, Adelaide, we must eat."

Vaguely, Adelaide registered the Cree words; she smelled willow smoke and grouse stew.

"Shall we camp here for a day or two?" Kid asked. "I have a canoe at the river. We can go to Yellowjacket Lake," he gestured and spoke.

"Ehe," said Adelaide. "I like." Two years before, Adelaide and Alex had fished in Yellowjacket Lake.

Adelaide, Kid, Dan, and the children walked down to the river where the canoe was stored, bottom up, and raised from the ground out of the reach of marauding bears. Together the men lifted it down and slid it into the water. By morning they would know whether it leaked and needed to be caulked.

The next morning, Adelaide, Dan, and the children canoed in leisurely fashion, following the twists and turns of the river. Adelaide saw startled ducks skim the water and rise into the air. She saw a family of timber wolves. Their eyes, so many eyes, watched. A caribou swam, and disappeared, and swam again. As the canoe approached, she saw nothing. Adelaide had expected to see the caribou lumber onto a safer shore, as it had before, but there was nothing to be seen.

They beached the canoe, Adelaide stepped out, caught Mosie as he jumped to shore, and then she took Mary in her arms and hugged her. Squirrels that had scolded before, scolded now. Adelaide, her children, and Dan followed the path to the lake. The same Wilson's warbler on the same branch, sang its cheery song.

Adelaide fashioned a pole for herself from a bit of willow, fastened a line and a hook, and baited it with a bit of gut she had saved from the grouse. She fixed another for Mosie, and one for Mary without the hook. They fished from a crude pole raft still there from last year. The same curious camp robber perched and flitted about. The sun shone down on them.

Adelaide and the children basked in the sun's warmth. They brushed off the hungry mosquitoes that came at sunset to torment them. Mosquitoes didn't worry Adelaide and her children.

When they returned, they constructed drying racks. Adelaide, with the children's help, gathered willow wood, and together, they built a fire. Then, she cleaned the fish and put them to smoke.

They camped over for a day, but on the morning of the next day, Kid said, "We should move on."

"Namoya!" Adelaide said.

"For Alex," Kid coaxed, but Adelaide bowed her head and sat. After a time, she rose, and together they packed and left.

First they forded the Yellowjacket, then they were on their way. As they travelled down the Canoe River, the country was no longer familiar to Adelaide. Alex and Kid had trapped up the Canoe River and Camp Creek, but the McCaulay family had only ventured as far as Yellowjacket Lake. Beyond the Yellowjacket, the going was easy enough until they forded another stream and found themselves in a large swamp. Miles of swamp had to be crossed; there was no way around. For the whole of the afternoon they struggled with the swamp, searching without result for easier routes. The bog was unremitting. The children rode uneasily, and intermittently, they walked. At times Adelaide or Kid carried Mary. Everyone else walked and tugged at horses.

The trail, much travelled by prospectors, was in bad shape, and the horses sunk to their knees or all the way to their chests. The men coaxed them through, alternately pulling, prodding, and pushing the less willing animals who seemed to sink the furthest and stick the hardest.

In the late afternoon, they were clear of the swamp. The river bank rose into Rat Rock, a sheer face named for the rock rabbits that inhabited it.

"We have to go until we reach the good pasture," Kid said. "A little while more. It's just across the next creek."

"Ehe," Adelaide said, but her heart told her to turn back. The children were exhausted.

They forded Bulldog Creek, a torrent now after the day of blazing sun. The horses floundered and swam, and all their gear was soaked. They rode on till they came to a swamp border with lush grass. On a bank above the swamp, someone had built a small cabin, and at this, they stopped. The children fell onto the bunk and slept.

Doggedly, she set about the familiar tasks: building a fire, mixing bannock, making tea. The men fetched water and gathered firewood, then unpacked the horses, put them to pasture, and once again, hung gear, bedding, and tents to dry. They erected one canvas fly between the pasture and the return trail and another between the pasture and the trail ahead. Dan and Bill would sleep under one without bedding but with a fire in front for warmth. They would listen for the bells of horses attempting to stray back on the trail. Kid would sleep under the other and listen for those trying to go ahead.

When they returned for their meal, they found Adelaide staring off into space beside a dying fire. The exhausted men prepared a meal of sorts and sat drinking tea.

"A trapper that was here a couple of years ago built a boat for trapping beaver in the swamp and along the river," Kid said. "We use it to go to the hot springs, just across the river. It is a great place. Adelaide could go there while we give the horses a day on good pasture."

Dan explained in Cree to Adelaide, and she nodded agreement. She would go alone. The children could stay with Dan and Kid. The next morning, as she rowed into the current, the children watched and waved hesitantly from the bank. She had promised them that she would return soon.

After crossing the river, she walked in a damp mist along a trail; it seemed she had stumbled into a tropical clime. Giant cow parsnip interspersed with fern obscured the path, while cedar and fir, rooted deep in the moss, towered above and screened out the sun. Devil's club vines, with creamy white flowers pyramiding on every side, curled out and grabbed at her legs; the pungent odor of skunk cabbage permeated the air.

A little further on, she stooped to admire a tiny pink flower with petals bent back from the bright yellow anthers—the bog cranberry. She marvelled again that its thread-like stem would later hold a pendulous berry—a delicious berry. As she mused she heard the tattoo of woodpeckers and the songs of many birds. She rose and continued on her way.

Where the trail ended, long grasses and bulrushes fringed a cold water lake and pond lilies floated. Out on the lake, ducks, loons, and grebe swam, and a kingfisher studied the water from its perch above. As she watched, she thought; she, too, could fish for her meal. She could gather roots of pond lily, bulrush, skunk cabbage; many different roots. She could gather flowers and buds of the river beauty and seeds of the sedge. Some of the stalks of the cow parsnip were still young and tender. If she had her children with her, they could survive here and eat well for the whole summer. They could harvest each thing in its season.

She continued over to the springs and looked down on the green algae blanketing the warm water of the springs and coating the logs that formed a tub where the water bubbled up. When Adelaide stepped forward and touched the water, a shaft of light filtered through the trees and the lit the moss and the water. She felt the spirits, the gentle spirits, all about her. She began to chant softly: her healing had begun.

Adelaide did not return the next day, nor the next. The men waited; they checked the horses' feet, rubbed a lame horse with liniment, and replaced a shoe on one of Cook's geldings. They fished, and they hunted. Kid began to worry about Adelaide, but Dan said not to worry. She would come when she was ready. On the third day, when Adelaide returned, her expression was soft and peaceful.

As they travelled on, they came upon Ptarmigan Creek which tumbled out of a canyon onto a broad flat. The raging torrent had dumped windfalls, roots, sand, and rocks in its path. The water had spread out over the flat and divided into five channels at its mouth. Here, the water was shallow, and the horses waded.

Beyond the creek, the river wound in a big 'S'. They came upon a long slough inhabited by beaver, muskrat, mink, marten, otter, and myriad water birds. Highbush cranberry, adorned with clusters of snow white flowers, thrived along the river bank and cottonwood, many of them felled by the beaver. Giant spruce, fir, and cedar flanked the swamp and the air was perfumed from a tiny species of orchid which rose in slender spires from the bog.

Across the river, the Ptarmigan Falls tumbled down a sheer rock face, and snow-peaked mountains enclosed the valley. Adelaide, enveloped in grandeur, reined in her horse and sat in silence.

They turned from the river to skirt the swamp and to travel on higher ground, and as they approached the Ptarmigan slide, they saw the pinkish sheen of a tiny delicate flower; the spring beauty was in full bloom. Among the flowers black grizzly bears were pawing and eating.

"Indian potato," Adelaide said. "Bear eat them. Us, too."

"The grizzlies can have them. I don't argue with grizzlies," Kid chuckled.

The evening was warm, and a soft breeze blew up from the river, and the bears, unaware of their presence, continued to feed. If the horses caught the bear's scent, they would spook. Cautiously, the riders continued on their way.

Toward evening, they came upon a tiny cabin located in an open meadow, their destination for that day. They unpacked and freed the horses for the night, and as Dan first shot grouse, then unpacked with the help of Bill, Adelaide chopped wood for the fire, and Kid took the children to help gather wood and to fish in the river. When they returned, the children snuggled close to their mother. They feasted on grouse, freshly caught Dolly Varden, and bannock.

The cabin sat among willow, birch, and aspen. That evening, they watched a herd of caribou cross the meadow and head for the timber. Kid quelled Dan's temptation to shoot by telling him of the mountain goat they were sure to see at the Goat Lick.

In the morning they continued on their way. Adelaide had resumed her share of responsibilities; her children tentatively tested her moods and her willingness to laugh with them and to tell stories. With three men able to give their full attention to the horses, the party continued on their way. They had travelled for over a week, and had only covered a third of the distance.

With Adelaide's help, they were able to travel faster at least over the good trail, but much swamp, steep trail, and rocks would be negotiated before they reached Donald.

The month of July was half gone when they finally rode up to the Sullivan River. Mosie, looking towards the pasture ahead, suddenly cried out, "Paul's here! Look! Sparky!" At the sound, the pony looked up, snorted, and galloped away with mane and tail flying.

As they watched, Adelaide and the children saw more horses, all familiar. Adelaide had known cousins, aunts, uncles, and some of her friends travelled through the mountains for hunting and fishing, but she had never accompanied them. Now, she realized this was the place. As they neared the campsite, they saw smoke from the campfire, and they saw teepees, men, women, children, and dogs.

As they rode into the camp, children and adults, recognizing them, ran to meet them. Tearful greetings followed.

"Alex?" someone asked.

Explanations followed, questions and answers. Kid and Bill were excluded, were not welcomed; they hung back and busied themselves with the horses.

Adelaide told of the trapping, the quarreling: "Hughes said we should go with him, but we wanted to go home. Alex was tightening the cinch," she explained. "He didn't know Hughes would shoot."

The white men received belligerent stares from men, women, and children.

Adelaide told them about tending Alex alone for days, about Dan coming, then Kid, about Kid tending Alex, about their long journey to report to the redcoats. Slowly, reluctantly the Métis accepted the two white men.

Kid and Bill stayed only an hour or two, long enough to have tea, rest the horses, and make sure Adelaide's clan would stay a while. Afterwhich, they travelled on toward Donald, and stopped for the night at Kid's cabin at Beavermouth.

"I'm flat broke," Bill Cook said. "I'll travel south, get a job. I'll write, let you know where I am."

Adelaide, Dan, and the children were within a day's travel from Donald, so they stayed at the Métis camp. A long night of mournful drumming, mournful chanting began.

Adelaide stayed with her kin for the balance of the summer. The relatives took her and her children into their tents, as was their custom, and provided for her needs. She picked berries, dried fish and meat, tanned caribou and deer hides. They spent the remaining weeks of the summer gathering food for the coming winter. Her children played with the other children who gathered berries and imitated other life skills of the parents.

Dan also stayed. He must interpret for Adelaide in the whiteman's court.

In the fall when snow threatened in the mountains, the Métis left before pasture was buried deep in snow. When the time came, they left, but Adelaide and Dan stayed. The Supreme Court trial was still to come.

Chapter XVI

For years, Kid Price told the story of the hearing in Donald and the trial in Golden. Around campfires, in lonely cabins, and in noisy bars, summer or winter, among prospectors and trappers, on the trail to Tête Jaune Cache and beyond, down the Fraser and up its tributaries, he told of the summer of '99. After a time, he thought of it less, but when it came to mind, he could still tell about it. When he was a hundred years old and in that old man's home in Victoria, people thought his mind was wandering. They didn't believe the trial could have ended the way it did. Not in Canada.

In late July of '99, two men paddling down the Columbia River in the pouring rain saw a log cabin with a window overlooking the river. Smoke curled from the lone stovepipe suggesting the inhabitant was home, so the men beached their canoe, and as they jumped ashore, a tall lanky man with a water pail in his hand came around the building and, striding toward them, dipped water from the river.

"Come on in out of the rain," the man said. "I'll have tea ready in a minute. Folks call me Kid."

"Buck," said the first man, and "Red," said his companion.

They walked toward a small cabin with long shakes on the roof, and as they rounded to the front, they saw that the roof extended to form a porch which was well stocked with firewood. On top of the firewood sat a gold pan, and in it were a prospector's hammer and a chisel. From a peg in the wall hung a number of traps. From a nail near another window that looked out onto the trail, a washtub and scrub-board hung. The door was of hewn plank.

Kid opened the door, stepped in, and placed the water pail on a shelf beside a washbasin and dipper. As the door opened, the men smelled the stew that was simmering on the stove, and as they entered, a pleasant scent of tobacco and of spruce fire. As their eyes adjusted to the light, they could see a pot-bellied stove on which the stew and a kettle boiled. A can of cigarette tobacco, cigarette papers, a pocket knife, an enameled cup, a coal-oil lamp, and an open book rested on a table in front of the window. A walnut chair with the back curved around into arms was pulled back from the table as if someone had just risen from it. Bits of the original dark varnish still clung to the chair. Another chair, homemade in the French Canadian style with a ladder back and woven rawhide seat, was pushed into the far end of the table. A bench of split log made a third seat. Against one wall a bunk made of split poles offered the comfort of feather pillows and grey woolen blankets.

The visitors first shed their soaked outer garments, hung them on a wire over the stove, and stood in their sagging underwear. Since the armchair seemed to be Kid's customary place, Buck chose the other chair, Red, the bench. Happy to be out of their tent on this wet day, the visitors relaxed and waited for their clothes to dry.

Kid stoked the fire, gathered enameled cups from pegs on the wall, and prepared to make tea. Buck retrieved a can of coffee from his pack, and Red, a bottle of rum, so the choice of drink changed to coffee with rum.

The can of milk had been open for several days, but Kid poured some into his brew. The guests waited to see if it would curdle. It didn't. They poured some into their drinks and added generous spoonfuls of sugar. While they drank, Kid made bannock and ladled grouse stew onto tin plates.

While Kid had his back turned dishing up the stew, Red spit on his knife, wiped it on the leg of his underwear and did the same with his fork.

The men had unloaded canoe and gear at Donald station and were going north. They had heard of the gold in Swift Current Creek, and they meant to try their luck. Kid warned them that they shouldn't believe all the rumours, and they assured him they didn't. They had been to the Yukon and had prospected there. When they returned, they heard about the gold at Tête Jaune Cache.

They had heard that the stream must be diverted, and they intended to build a cabin, prepare for the dig, and wait for shallow water in early autumn. They would prospect into the winter and then trap until they could come out in the spring.

Kid told them that he knew the gold was there—but you couldn't get at it in the hot summer when the glaciers melted. Then, you wouldn't find colour one pan in ten. But when the weather turned cold, when the water washed the stream bed, there was colour in every pan, not enough to pay, but they were lookig for the source. When someone found the source, there would be enough for everyone.

As they finished their dinner, Kid said he had no heart for prospecting at the moment. He would be taking Doc north to do an autopsy as soon as the doctor was ready.

"You know about the murder then," Buck said, more a statement than a question.

Kid placed the rice paper between the fingers of his right hand, added a generous pinch of tobacco, deftly rolled the cigarette with one hand, lit a match, placed the cigarette between his lips, and drew a deep breath. Buck lifted the tin lid from a small round cardboard container, curled his index finger around the inside, deposited snuff under his lower lip, replaced the lid, and settled back to listen. Red took a plug of tobacco and a knife from his pocket, pared off a portion, placed it under his lip, and sucked. When Kid had smoked his cigarette to a butt that burned his fingers, he got up lifted the stove lid and dropped it in.

"I didn't bring the prisoner in, he said. Jack Evans did. I stayed with Alex till he died, you know. Then Dan Noyes and I brought the widow in. She was the only witness, you see."

"Holy Mary!" You were there," Red interrupted. "What really happened?"

Kid gave a run through of the horrors of the murder and of the condition of the family when he arrived.

"We had our doubts about the story we heard in the town," Red commented. "Sounded too pat."

"When I got to town after leaving Adelaide and Dan at Sullivan River, folks were expecting me. Jack and the boys got to Donald about a week ahead of me.

"The boys?" Red interjected. "And weren't they all for going to Edmonton?"

"Yes! But Jack had convinced Joe Hostyn, Henry Hollings, and Sam Derr to do the trip to Golden. They were going for supplies, and Golden is two thirds the distance compared with Edmonton. Even after I was there looking after Alex, Dan refused to leave his friend, so they lost one guide for the trip east. If they went to Golden, they would be paid for bringing in a prisoner."

"Oh yes! And that would change their minds." Red nodded and grinned.

"They expected to give testimony because they were the first to the scene of the crime, and they could do this and avoid another trip out. Helping Jack with his prisoner was an easy choice for those prospectors.

When Jack and his companions arrived in Donald, Griffith . . . he's the stipendiary magistrate. Griffith held the preliminary hearing. That was in Donald. Donald is pretty well a ghost town as you probably noticed. There's no more rail construction. The courthouse and the jail are still in Donald, but they'll be moved to Golden some time this summer.

Before Jack left Swift Current Creek, he took measurements and made diagrams of the scene of the shooting. He took Hughes' rifle, Alex's hat pierced by the bullet, and Alex's bloody shirt. He even took a piece of Alex's jaw bone."

"It sounds bloody awful."

"Well, we wanted to be sure there was enough evidence to hang the bugger. We've travelled that trail often enough to know it's a long way back."

Buck said, "How in hell did they travel with that trigger happy nut? They had to sleep some time."

"Jack didn't have any problems bringing in his prisoner. Hughes don't see nothing wrong with shooting an Indian, but he wouldn't shoot a white man. No! Hughes was no problem. He was going to show the law that he was a good boy and done them a favour.

"But Hughes' horses were another matter. They are as thick-headed as he is, and they were trouble.

"Jack wanted Hughes to leave his outfit at the camp, but the stubborn old bugger wouldn't. He'd have left them, by God, if I was taking him out. After spending all those days watching Alex die, I'd have handcuffed him and tied him to the saddle. I'd probably have shot him, too, long before I got to Donald.

"Anyway, Jack took Hughes' horses, too. That made three strings, all strange to each other, a total of twenty horses with almost nothing to pack.

"Jack's string was heading home; they followed his saddle horse willingly enough. But the other two strings were just ornery and fought, kicked, and bit the whole damn way.

"Sam's string on their own wouldn't be too bad. He had bought them from one herd near Edmonton; they had travelled together all their lives. Two men could lead a horse each, you see, while the third followed behind herding them alone, keeping them together. Well, that wasn't the way it worked. Hughes' string was next after Jack's. Jack wanted to keep Hughes where he could watch him, you see. Hostyn came next, and tried to keep the strings separated. Every time one of the horses fell back the nag behind bit it, and it kicked back. Next, Henry Hollings led a reluctant animal, and a few more followed whenever they weren't fighting. Sam Derr tended to keep as far from Hughes as he could, so he rode at the rear leading a filly that shied every time a branch broke or a grouse flew up.

"If Hughes had left his outfit, it would have made more sense. John Smith, at the Bonanza Mine, hauls supplies in and hauls mica out by pack horse, over two hundred miles to Kamloops. He'll pay a good price for horses and supplies there at the end of the trail. Hughes found out he needed money when he got to Golden: Jack hadn't told him. Jack wanted Hughes to travel willingly, and I suppose he was right.

"For the first day, they followed the trail toward Kamloops, down the Fraser River to the crossing at Tête Jaune and on to our camp at Starvation Flats where they stopped for the rest of the day. After a quick meal, Jack left the boys to clean up and split wood. Jack expected them to replace what they'd used; you know. He went into the garden. The hoe was in the garden where I left it when the prospectors came for us."

"You mean he stopped to tend the garden?" Buck asked.

"Yep! That's Jack. He hilled the potatoes and pulled every weed. He would be gone for a month or more, and we needed that garden, murderer be damned. He was sick of eating beans for ten months of the year, and so was I."

"A good country lad, that Jack," Red commented.

"Guess he just stacked his prisoner in a corner and went to work," Buck laughed.

"The next morning, they travelled through Starvation Flats and along the trail from Bonanza Mine. It was almost the end of June, and Smith had been hauling mica since spring, so the trail was a mess. Most of Starvation Flats is barren; pretty, you understand, but barren—jackpine, lichen, and sand.

"Wherever a long train of horses hoofs had slashed the lichen into shreds, the horses sunk with every step into the shifting sand. Jack reined his mount around a scrawny pine and carved a new trail. Instead of following, the horses fanned out all over the place, and the boys chased after them. Hughes was supposed to be a prisoner, but he was as busy as anyone throughout the trip. Like I told you, he had a string of horses that were as ornery as him.

"The trail gets better when you get closer to Swift Creek. Kinnikinnik and cranberry plants cover the sand, and so the ground is firmer. When you skirt Cranberry Lake, there's a swampy stretch. No way around that. The mountain rises right up from the lake, but the bog is corduroyed. The trail divides shortly after you pass the lake. They veered south towards the Canoe River. The valley is wide and wet. Huge mountains go right up into the snow on the west side. It's thick with timber where the trail is; pine, spruce, fir, cedar, rocky ledges, devil's club, and swamps infested with mosquitoes. That's the Canoe Valley.

"I've travelled there myself in every season. I think summer is the worst. Mosquitoes, horseflies, sandflies, and no-see-ums. If I'd a' been taking Hughes, I'd a' stripped him and tied him to a tree. But Jack took him on."

The men had listened attentively to the description of that trail, but finally Red interrupted again. "And why is the trail there at all? Wouldn't paddling the rivers be easier?"

Kid walked over, stoked the fire, and added water and more coffee to the pot. Then, he returned to his seat.

"Nope! Not at all! Canoe River eats canoes in the spring. It's okay this time of year and in the fall if you're a good boatman. Plenty of rapids on the Columbia, too. Watch for them even in the summer. It's a graveyard for some mother's sons. Let me tell you.

"Anyhow, the government gave us eight hundred to upgrade that trail, because of the gold, you see. But pack-trains wore it out. Before crossing the worst of the swampy areas, the boys stopped and laid more corduroy. They hope to use that trail before it gets worn out again. And Jack intended to get enough work out of Hughes and his horses to pay for the bother they caused.

"There are a lot of creeks, some more like rivers in the summer. During the heat of the day, they get too high, and sometimes the boys camped for half a day and the night waiting to ford in the cool of the morning. Run-off is always bad that time of year. Creeks you wouldn't notice most times are torrents. The boys spent a lot of time swapping tales over the camp fire, fishing, and shooting game while they waited for a better time to cross—altogether, a slow trip.

"They met a stream of prospectors along the way; some with good outfits, saddle and pack horses, some afoot leading their one pack-horse, and some that thought they could pack a summer's supplies on their own backs. River was in flood; nobody was boating.

"Everyone thinks Tête Jaune will be the next Dawson City, you know. And it will. But it'll break many a greenhorn before we find the motherlode.

"Jack and the boys caught up with Archdeacon McKay who was returning to Golden. His companions had long since deserted him. He had run out of grub and was on his way home, but when Jack told him about the shooting, he bummed some food off the boys. Said he must go back and help the poor man.

"Have you met the Archdeacon?"

"No! Can't say I have. At home, we don't seek for Church of England men."

"Well, the Archdeacon is different than most," Kid grinned. "He might just be your kind of guy. He was baptizing, marrying, and burying at Golden, but he got bored. He quit and went to the Yukon gold rush. That was the spring of '97. When he returned last fall, he promised the missus he wouldn't leave her and the children again. He makes that promise often and he means it every time, but gold beckons.

"Ten of Golden's citizens raised one hundred dollars between them, and in March, the Archdeacon and his party left Golden with dogs and toboggans. They were on their way to the Tête Jaune gold rush, and they didn't want anybody there ahead of them.

"By the time the Archdeacon bought dogs, toboggans, grub, and a bottle of rum, there wasn't much of that hundred left to feed the wife and the wee ones. The best citizens of Golden send their little ones to Mrs. McKay, so she gets paid for piano lessons, but the poor woman is skinny as a crow, and the Archdeacon isn't back yet. Well, that's the Archdeacon."

"No! Can't say I've met his kind. Our priests are married to Mother Church, and they don't neglect her at all," Red offered.

Kid grinned and continued, "Transportation of that prisoner was damn casual, but at the end of the trip Evans faced the serious business of turning Hughes over to the law. At Wait-a-Bit Creek there is pasture, so he left Hughes there with the boys and the horses while he rode on to Donald. Jack reported the shooting to Sheriff Redgrave. He delivered Hughes' rifle, Alex's hat with bullet hole, Alex's bloody shirt, the piece of Alex's jaw bone, and the diagrams of the scene. Jack told the sheriff Alex was still alive when he left but wasn't likely to survive."

"Redgrave?" Buck asked. "Not the same that brought the Overlanders through the Yellowhead Pass?"

"The very same. Redgrave was a hardy soul when he came into the country, but he is getting a mite old. He doesn't relish a long ride. He got Stirrett to ride back with Jack and take Hughes in. Hughes was charged with attempt murder, and Griffith held a prelim to see if they should stick him in jail. When O'Brien heard, he was right there, bright as a new penny. They didn't know Alex had died, but O'Brien could smell opportunity.

"In court, Jack said that Hughes had given him no trouble on the way out. Jack told Griffith how we first heard of the shooting. He described Alex's wounds and the shape he was in when we got there. He told about going into Hughes' tent and taking the guns.

"Then O'Brien questioned him, and Jack explained how he told Hughes that he should come to Golden, and Hughes agreed to come. O'Brien asked if Alex could talk. He asked all about that. The fool doesn't understand that it doesn't always take words to talk. I know O'Brien was trying to trip the boys up on something, and I guess we'll find out at the trial what it is. I sure don't trust that bugger."

Kid stopped and added another stick to the fire. The visitors went to the door and spat their chews onto the ground. Buck went around the corner to pee. Red poured rum all around, and Kid added coffee. The men sipped at their drinks and settled down to listen again. Kid rolled another cigarette, smoked it, and took healthy gulps from his drink. He warmed to his topic.

"Henry Hollings took the witness stand and this is the way he saw it."

Kid's eyes narrowed. He pulled his elbows in, hunched his back, and peered around suspiciously. He spoke with a whiny nasal twang.

"When we arrived at Swift Current Creek, we saw a tent and teepee over the other side of the stream. We started to unpack, when we saw a woman waving. She seemed upset, so Mr. Hostyn went across to see what was the matter. Joe, Mr. Hostyn that is, can't speak Indian, so he called Dan. Noyes, that is. When Dan got over there and talked to Mrs. McCaulay, he didn't even come back to tell us; like he should have. He just hollered, 'Alex is shot!' Then he headed for the teepee. We unpacked our pack horses and swam our saddle horses across and went to see the wounded man.

"On our way, we met Mr. Hughes. He recognized me and shook hands with me, and I introduced him around to the rest of the boys. Mr. Hughes said, 'You better go in and look at him and see what you think of him.'

"We went in, and McCaulay seemed to recognize us. He crossed himself as if he wanted us to pray for him, so I left."

"So! And what would be his problem?" Red asked.

Kid made a wry face, shook himself, rested his elbows on the arms of his chair, and sitting back, he said, "Henry Hollings was in court, you see. He didn't want to be charged for consorting with a Dougan."

Red jumped to his feet, his muscles tense and his eyes flashing. "I'll consort with him or anyone that wants some consorting." He spit the words through his teeth.

Kid made a down motion with his hand. "Hold on, lad!" he said. " I consider you a friend. If you really want to fight, keep your fists polished for the likes of Hughes and his friends."

Kid drained his cup, rolled another cigarette and took a few puffs, and Red returned hesitantly to his seat.

"What about the murder? How did he explain Hughes there?" Buck asked.

Kid puffed for a while and then put his cigarette down. Again, his voice and his pose changed, elbows in, hunched shoulders, suspicious gaze. His voice acquired a whine.

"I asked Jim, 'What made you shoot the boy, Jim?' and Jim said, 'I supplied his whole damn family with grub all the way up, and he wanted to get away with all the fur and the rest of my grub. He threatened to lay a lickin' on me. I heard a shot.'

"Of course you know, it may have been one of the children throwing a cartridge into the fire, but Mr. Hughes didn't know that.

"Then I said, 'Jim. You might have thought of the woman and children, and got even with him some other way.'

"Mr. Hughes agreed with me and shook his head sadly. He said, 'Yes, Henry! How I wish I had.'

"I told Mr. Hughes I thought the best thing for him to do was go out with Jack; Mr. Evans, that is. I reminded him about the Moberlys. They're sons of Henry Moberly and a native woman, and they look after their kind around Henry House. They would be riding through the pass. We were afraid they would create a disturbance.

"Next morning he left the camp with us and Jack."

Kid paused, rested his elbows on the arms of the chair, and leaned forward earnestly. His hands were fists. He snorted.

"Hollings, Hostyn, and Hughes, those three talked things over all the way down. By the time Hughes reached the court-room, they all believed he was as innocent as a lamb. Jack told me later, they didn't talk in front of him and Sam. Jack thought Hughes had got himself in enough trouble. I'd see that man hanged and gladly, but Jack has no stomach for it. In court, it sounded as if Jack thinks the same as the rest.

"You know Sam Derr? He guides, does some outfitting. You'll meet him when you go north. Fine fellow! Sam limited his testimony to what happened after he came on the scene. He has no love for Hughes, but he couldn't be hard on a man that is facing the gallows.

"He told the magistrate, 'By what I understand from conversation with Mrs. McCaulay, Alex and Hughes quarreled over a saddle or beaver skins.' He wasn't asked any more questions, so that is all he got the chance to say.

"But Joe Hostyn—he is a man of opinion. He hadn't seen any more than Jack or Sam, but somehow he knew what happened."

Kid dropped his hands to his lap, sat erect, and tilted his head. His voice had acquired a dogmatic tone.

"Mister Hughes said he heard some noise. It may have been the children throwing a shell into the fire, but he wasn't sure. McCaulay had threatened to lay a lickin' on him. Hughes jumped to his feet and took his gun. He thought McCaulay was picking up his cinch rope and making for him, so he shot.

"These three men had their say, accepted their pay, and left. But before they left, Hollings and Hostyn spread their opinions in every bar in Golden. The prosecutor should have a chance to have a go at them. Their testimony isn't evidence, but it sure created sympathy for that rat in the coop. Word spread like wildfire on the street. In homes, restaurants, hotels, and bars throughout the valley, it was the talk of the season. And then, it was written up in *The Golden Era*. I've got a copy here.

"*Attempted Murder*," Kid read to his guests. "*Victim Not Likely to Recover.*"

He read of the attempt to murder a young quarter-breed, Alex McCaulay, by an old man, Jim Hughes. The two were trapping, he read, but when the men went to divide up the furs they quarreled. Hughes had done all the work and brought supplies for the McCaulays; Alex, his half-breed wife, and two children, but McCaulay wanted the whole of the season's catch and threatened Hughes.

He read of the damage done by the bullet and of the prospectors coming upon the wounded man who had lain for nine days unable to eat.

Kid continued to read: "Further particulars go to show that when the shooting occurred, McCaulay was packing up to leave. He was bending by his horse to pick up the cinch of the pack saddle, with his head towards Hughes when the latter fired using a .45-.90 rifle."

A description of the wounds followed. Mrs. McCaulay was credited with keeping Alex alive till help arrived.

The Golden Era reported that Jim Hughes behaved himself splendidly on the seventeen day trip out. The article closed with the statement:

Hughes took the matter very coolly, digging a grave for his victim and going to the teepee every morning to ask Mrs. McCaulay whether Alex was yet dead.

"Well, yes," commented Red. "And that's a mulligan to fill a glutton."

"Yes, and you can be sure the boys at the bar slavered over the choicest tidbits. Hughes refused to testify. Said that he reserved his testimony for the supreme court, but the court and the town had already heard his version through his buddies.

"But, let them talk. We'll take Doc to Tête Jaune for the autopsy. He'll bring back all the proof that's needed.

"You know, it is getting late. You fellows probably want an early start. You can bed down on the floor or you can go into the hay mow with your bedroll. The hay mow is softer than the floor, and it will be warmer than your tent. Come in for bannock and tea in the morning."

Very early the next morning, the men awoke. The sun was just peeking over the mountains when Kid called his guests for breakfast, and it had not risen far when the two prospectors climbed into their Peterborough canoe and paddled northward. Kid watched until they were out of sight. He turned to enter his cabin, and then turned again and gazed longingly at the water flowing north.

Chapter XVII

Their trip to Butchart Gardens rained out, Alan treated his mother and uncle to dinner. They settled back to tea, a light dessert, and their favourite topic; Percy's adventures. Clara and Alan asked the occasional question or made comment, but mostly Percy carried the conversation.

"Can you imagine the stew Griffith was in when I arrived and told him McCaulay died? He paid Jack and friends for bringing in Hughes and then me, for bringing in the chief witness. Now, he had to send the doctor a couple hundred miles to do an autopsy. That would take a month. The Attorney-General had not requested him to hold Jack and the boys as witnesses so that saved a bundle. Still, he knew the whole thing would cost more than his year's salary. Hell! More than his year's budget. As government agent, he knew how popular that would be in Victoria.

"British Columbia, then, was like California thirty years earlier. Everybody that came, the premiers, judges, lawyers, doctors, speculators, miners, even the poorest panhandlers, came for the same reason I did, to find gold. Folks wanted railroads, trails and bridges. Investors in Britain willingly poured in the money, and every government elected borrowed all they could.

"The government owed over a million dollars, and those British investors had decided it was time they got something back. Taxes and royalty both went up. Politicians didn't belong to parties then. They were on their own, and support depended on which way the wind blew. Governments tumbled every few months.

"The whole town of Golden grew because the railroad opened the Canadian Rockies for prospecting. Haggen run the paper. Called it *The Golden Era*, he did. He was a mining engineer, and came all the way from Australia for gold, and by God, he found it. He joined the Golden Board of Trade. He became a notary public, conveyancer, mining, real estate, and finance agent, and found purchasers for prospects and development claims. Haggen printed every rumour. Gold didn't have to exist in those claims. He could dig it out, regardless.

"In the same paper that told about the shooting, the headline in boxcar letters read, *Golden To Tête Cache*. Underneath was a map that covered half the page—the route to the Tête Jaune Cache placer claims on Swift Current Creek. Beside the map was a lurid report of the shooting, and below that, a blown up story about the advantage of the trail from Golden to the Tête Jaune over the trail from Kamloops. Then a report about Jack, the boys, their twenty pack-horses, and their trip from Tête Jaune Cache.

"Haggen blamed the lack of news about gold on the high water that prevented prospecting. He said Jack and I had done some prospecting and found some promising quartz. True enough, but somehow every flake of gold we found got converted into a gold mine.

"The item went on to say the men had seen Archdeacon McKay and told him about the shooting and the archdeacon turned about and went back. Haggen speculated, 'whether it was news of better gold prospects or a desire to help the injured man, McCaulay, was not known—probably the latter.' And you can bet, everybody thought the former.

"The story closed saying, 'The party of four intended to outfit and return.'

"Outfit and return!" Percy snorted. "That's what Haggen was interested in. Haggen printed stories about the north and about gold. He printed Alex's story with every sensational detail because that got people reading. He didn't give a damn about

Alex or the hell Adelaide suffered. He was in the business of promoting a gold rush."

Percy went to the cupboard and dug out a sheaf of newspapers, ragged, brittle, and yellow with age.

"I'd been warning men that we hadn't found that much gold in Tête Jaune, and in May of '99, I went to Haggen and told him. Here's what he wrote. Read it. Haggen quotes me."

In a brief article Kid Price was quoted: "I am sorry to hear of the reports that have been circulated from Edmonton through Mr. Jackson's correspondence as to the richness of the field, for there has been nothing developed so far to justify any such sensational reports. The story about $40 a day being taken out is nonsense, for there has not been a dollar's worth of gold yet sent from the ground."

"Well! It does sound as if he let you give men fair warning," Alan said.

"Indeed he did, but read this. Which do you think men believed?"

In the same paper Mr. Haggen printed the Dominion Geologist's report about Tête Jaune Cache. It filled two full length columns. He had prefaced the report with seven different headlines: *Tête Jaune Cache, A Country of Interest, Dominion Geologists Report, Highest Peak of The Rockies, A Great Valley, Gold and Silver Fields, Wonderful Mica Deposits.*

Almost an entire column was given over to a description of the valley, both its beauty and its geological diversity. The magnificence of Mount Robson, the Fraser River, the Grand Forks, and Swift Current Creek was extolled. Tourmaline, garnet, cyanite, beryl, apatite, and mica are mentioned as well as gold and silver. The activity at the Bonanza mine, located on Mica Mountain, near Tête Jaune Cache, was reported, stating that J.F. Smith extracted sheets of mica eleven by eighteen inches, and sent them by packhorse to the rail at Kamloops, a distance of 215 miles.

The article continued:

A great hindrance to the development of this, or any other mining industry in this part of the country, is the difficulty of travelling without proper trails.

The mica mine and claims, in the Tête Jaune area, were all in the mountains on the west side of the valley which, according to the report, contained no gold. However, most of the streams on the other side showed colour. The rocks contained numerous quartz veins of a thickness of one to five feet. These quartz veins, it said, showed a good deal of oxidized iron-pyrites and some galena.

"Look!" Kid said and pointed to the page, "The rest of the paper makes it sound like we're getting gold by the shovelful. No man with blood in his veins could resist. Those who didn't buy a gold pan, grubstake, and pack horses, or a canoe, bought claims someone else had staked. The Golden Board of Trade badgered Wells, the M. P. P., to get money for trails, and I didn't mind that. The gold is there someplace, and I wanted to find it. Everybody wanted to find it. I just think folks should have gone with their eyes open.

"The Board of Trade asked for $2,000.00, but Premier Semlin gave them $800.00. With that money, The Golden Board of Trade managed to get us prospectors to upgrade eighty miles of trail and repair bridges. $2,000 would have got us all the way to Tête Jaune Cache. Sure it looked fine for us until the rush came. Then the trail was in worse shape than ever.

"At the first sign of spring, hordes started for the north, but first, they mailed clippings from *The Golden Era* to their relatives in the east. Brothers, cousins, and friends desert farms and fish-boats and join in the rush. In Golden they bought horses, gear, ammunition, supplies, everything they could afford. Golden was booming, and Golden merchants were as happy as clams. They even gave dozens of prospectors supplies on jaw-bone, and they paid for advertising in *The Golden Era*, and Haggen continued to blow up the gold rush.

"And all the while, those sweethearts in the east waited faithfully. Wives tended babies, gardens, cows, pigs, and chickens, and prayed that their men returned safely. Older sons ran away to join Papa and left the chores to the ones too young to run.

"Haggen quoted me, whatever I said. He knew everyone would hear it anyhow. But he sure made a fool of me when he didn't like what I said. Reading *The Golden Era* was like entering a house of distorted mirrors. I looked but couldn't recognize what I'd seen, done, or said. After the people of Golden read the geological report, everyone thought I was hiding something," Percy continued. "In June Haggen wrote, 'The secret of Price's rapid return to the Cache is out. He has evidently written A. Stewart, of Edmonton, stating he was going back to locate gold quartz. At least this is the statement of the *Edmonton Bulletin*.'

"Well you should have heard the rumours. Folks whispered around town that I came from Jesse James' Gang, and slipped into Canada in the spring of 1883. That was just a year after Jesse James was shot. It bothered folks that I lived a private life, looked happy, and only came to town when I had to. 'That guy has his secrets,' they said. I proved that I had, too. I applied for my Canadian citizenship and got it.

"But the thing that rankled the big boys in town the most was that Premier Semlin had spent money on trails for us, and I hadn't found gold. Griffith's boss, Mr. Henderson, had just been appointed as attorney-general by Premier Semlin to replace Joseph Martin who had been getting uppity. But Martin could afford to be uppity. He had plenty of supporters. Premier Semlin was scrambling for support wherever he could get it, and he needed to say that we had found gold.

"Had the man shot been a prospector far from home, and had the incident suggested a threat to prospectors, the expense might have been acceptable. He might have gained some support, but had we struck gold his election would be a cinch. However, Griffith was the magistrate, and he had to uphold the law, expense be damned. He had to conducted the preliminary hearings—two of them, the one charging Hughes with attempted murder, and now, another charging him with murder.

"I heard he grubstaked a couple of prospectors. He must have been desperate."

As Percy finished, the waiter placed the bill to Alan's left. The three had finished their tea, and rose to leave.

❖

Griffith typed the date on a letter he was about to write, July 10, 1899. He addressed his missive:

to The Honourable Alexander Henderson, Attorney General, Victoria. Sir,

I herewith enclose original depositions in Evans v Hughes, the charge being that of shooting with intent to kill.

He noted the distance, one hundred and sixty miles, a seventeen day trip to the scene of the crime. He continued:

"It would, of course, be impossible to bring the prisoner in alone. . . The trip occupied 17 days, and it will, of course, take them the same to return. I shall be glad to know at an early date what allowance . . .

He requested further instructions. He noted that McCaulay was not expected to live, and asked whether the men should be held over till the trial.

Griffith sat back and read his letter. He hoped the letter contained sufficient warning. He thought for a while, then he continued to write.

In closing, he considered it politic to mention that McCaulay was a quarter-breed, his wife a half-breed who spoke Cree only, and Hughes an American citizen.

On Friday of the same week, he received the approval of the office of the attorney general, and paid out the following moneys for the deliverance of the prisoner:- J. W. Evans, $184.10; J. Hostyn, $112.00; S. Derr, $80.00; H. Hollings, $80.00; J. Stirrett, $8.60; for a total of $464.70. The Attorney General did not advise him to hold the witnesses till the trial.

Griffith thoughtfully looked at that total. His salary for a year was $1200.00. Joe Stirrett, mining recorder and clerk, received $50.00 per month, but only for the months that he worked. By comparison, the outlay for this case was already considerable, and because of the distances involved, if Alex McCaulay died, huge expenses loomed.

He was not long in discovering his fears were well founded. On Monday, Kid Price arrived and reported the death to him. On Friday July 21, it was recorded in *The Golden Era*:

TETE JAUNE CACHE TRAGEDY
– Death of McCaulay –

Mr. Price, partner of J. W. Evans, arrived in Golden on Monday night with the news that McCaulay, who was shot at Tête Jaune Cache by Hughes, died on the 24th, nine days after the shooting. Price then buried the body and erected a fence round the grave and a cross over it. He then came out bringing with him the widow and two children. They had a very hard trip owing to the high water.

Mrs. McCaulay has been left at Sullivan River, Price coming ahead with the information for the Government Agent. Price managed to extract half of the bullet from the wounded man but could not find the remainder. The widow will be the principal witness at the trial of Hughes, which will be arranged for shortly. On Wednesday, Price returned to Sullivan River for Mrs. McCaulay.

On the same page Griffith read two articles that interested him:

This morning, Frank Bethune returned from Tête Jaune Cache and put in an appearance at the ERA office. He asked us to warn people against going to Tête Jaune Cache after placer gold. He says there is nothing there to justify the inrush. . . .'Why,' said Frank, 'you have a hundred times better prospects for placer gold on Canyon Creek within five miles of Golden and on Cummins Creek. Then again, even if there were gold on Swift Current, it would cost $5 to take out every dollar as the creek is filled with impossible boulders.

Owing to one of his horses getting entangled with a rope in crossing one of the creeks near Kinbasket Lake it was drowned and Frank lost his camp outfit.

The second article was a quote from the *Edmonton Bulletin*:

Interest in the Tête Jaune Cache gold excitement, which has been on the wane of late, is being revived. Jackson & McLaughlin have outfitted afresh at Golden and gone back, and R. Matz left for Donald to arrange for the immediate return to the Tête Jaune area of Joe Hostyn and Sam Derr who were sent in by him and some Edmonton men last year. These men brought out word that has not been made public but which is of sufficient importance to cause their immediate return.

Then Griffith read a quote from the *Kamloops Standard* which told of Harry Heath who had just returned from the Tête Jaune Cache and Fort George country where he had been prospecting. Mr. Heath intended to write a book about it.

Griffith shrugged at that bit of trivia, and then he returned to his problem. Mr. Price had reported to him on Monday afternoon, and Griffith must start the preparations for the preliminary hearing. If enough evidence surfaced, he would be charged with murder. An autopsy was the first necessity.

Chapter XVIII

When Griffith approached Dr. Taylor with the request that he do an autopsy on the body of Alex McCaulay, Dr. Taylor sat back in his swivel chair. The chair rolled away from his desk, and he looked out at fluffy white clouds nestled against the distant mountains. He looked down at his strong hands, the nails neatly trimmed, the skin as soft as the softest leather.

"I'd be a whole month on the trail." He looked up and laughed. "I'd need gloves or these hands would blister from holding the reins."

He sobered and continued. "Golden would be without a doctor while I was gone. There is one baby due in early September. If the labour starts early, Mrs. Conner could see to that. But there could be emergencies."

"In that case, we will see that the patient is transported to Field or Revelstoke. That is what was done before you came. We'll manage," Griffith assured him.

"There could be too much delay. I don't know." Dr. Taylor gazed out the window again, looked down at his clenched fists, then looked up again. "I don't know," he said again.

On July 31st, Dr. Taylor put his left hand on the saddle horn, his left foot into the stirrup, and swung onto the horse, and together with Jack Evans and Kid Price, started on a journey into the north country to perform an autopsy on the body of Alexander McCaulay.

Run-off was long over and the creeks were lower and easier to ford, but the horses sometimes sunk to their knees where the corduroy was buried in mud. When the horses mired down; they covered very few miles in a day, but the doctor was as happy as the day was long. He was the first up in the morning. He went, found his horse, petted it, gave it oats, and petted it some more.

Because of heavy rain, they sat in their tents for two days. No problem for Dr. Taylor. Kid told stories. The doctor listened.

They made it to Swift Current Creek the evening of August 15th. Next day was hot. Alex had been two months dead when Kid and Jack dug him up.

Even before they opened the coffin, the stench of rotted flesh assailed them. When they pried off the lid, Kid staggered away. He leaned against a tree, and heaved. He thought about the way Alex died, and he cried, "We had no right to dig him up."

Jack sniffed, blinked, wiped his eyes, and built a smudge to discourage the flies. While the men dug, the doctor had prepared a carbolic acid solution. He washed his hands in that and carefully scrubbed around his nails. He dipped a thin linen cloth in a clean solution and covered his nose and mouth. His holiday was over. With firm resolution, he began to cut. Above the mask, his face could be seen to turn increasingly grey, his eyes to show strain. Methodically he continued.

After a time as the doctor worked, Kid dipped his handkerchief into a solution, covered his nose and mouth, and returned to the doctor's side. The doctor continued to work until, suddenly, his hand dropped and staggered away from the putrid body. He removed his mask, breathed deeply, took a short walk, returned, and picked up his pen. He wrote: 'Patient in an emaciated condition, his body now much decomposed.' He turned to the cadaver and continued to probe.

The doctor pointed along the course of the bullet for Kid. "The bullet entered here and destroyed the eye socket," he said. He showed Kid where it went through the face to where it came through the skin and then re-entered. "Here," he said, "it punctured the pericardium, the sac containing the heart."

"Mostly, I had figured it out when I was looking after Alex," Kid said, "but some things still confused me. I wanted to hear what you had to say."

When he came to Alex's belly, he indicated the cut Kid had made. "The bullet didn't do that," he said.

"The bullet carried some matter along with it," Kid explained. "I had to take it out. The wound was infected and swollen. I had to poultice it before I could find the bullet. It was just under the skin. I could feel it. I made a little cut, about half an inch. The bullet came out easy."

The doctor walked away from the corpse, removed his mask, and breathed deeply. "This is the first time I have examined a decayed body. I hope it is also the last. I have never felt so ill." He sighed, took another gulp of fresh air, completed his notes, and went for a long walk.

When Dr. Taylor returned he said, "The bullet went through his mouth and would have gathered bacteria there. He would have been badly infected before you saw him." After a pause, the doctor remarked, "The man must have suffered terribly."

"I gave him morphine," Kid said.

"You did what you could," the doctor answered. "I doubt anyone could have saved him. Not here. Not without a hospital."

The autopsy took half a day. The return trip to Golden took twelve days, and on September 5, Magistrate Griffith held the preliminary hearing. There was enough evidence, and James Hughes was charged with murder.

Finishing a fine dinner, Percy mused: "Yes, Doc really enjoyed that trip. When he rode down the Columbia River past Kinbasket Lake, I remember what he said: 'I've listened to you fellows tell of your adventures ever since I came here. Never thought I'd get the chance. You know,' he continued, 'I try to worry. Some poor chap might break his neck while I'm gone, but I just don't care.'

"Before Jack and I could leave with Doc. I had to make sure Adelaide stayed in the valley until the hearing. No Redcoats had spoken to her, and she expected Redcoats," Percy said. "She might leave. She'd stay with her kin while they stayed, but she'd return with them when they left. I knew that. As soon as they saw new snow on the peaks, they'd be gone. Plenty of fish, game and berries, but there was no winter pasture. In that narrow valley, snow got too deep for the horses to paw.

"Dan was determined that Hughes hang. Maybe he'd convince her to stay if the rest left. And then I thought, 'Huh! We'll borrow Adelaide's pack horses. Adelaide would rather ride back alone than leave without her horses.' "

After finishing dinner, Clara, Percy, and Alan had returned to the residence, and at the urging of his nephew, Percy continued the tale which had accompanied that dinner.

Alan was particularly fascinated with the doctor's adventure in the mountains. "My God!" he said. "Dr. Taylor performed such a thorough autopsy on a cadaver two months dead. It is difficult to understand his stamina."

"Yes! Doc had stamina. That is for sure. While I puked, and Jack removed himself from the scene, Doc rolled up his sleeves and went to work."

Percy continued to tell about the autopsy. When he paused in the telling, Clara interrupted. "Tell me more about the doctor. Mind how far it was to a doctor when we were little?" Clara said. "Mama did most of the doctoring. I never saw a doctor 'til my third baby."

Percy laughed, "Dr. Taylor was only twenty-two when he first came from Ottawa in '93, to be the only doctor at the new hospital in Golden. He was tall, athletic, sandy haired, and had a mustache—very handsome. He played soccer and curled, and all the ladies turned out to watch, but I don't think he would have been much help at the birthing. He hadn't delivered many babies. You had Mama, a good midwife, and the ladies in Golden had Mrs. Conner, who had delivered the babies before the doctor came and the doctor depended on her.

"Doc was very thorough and a good practical man. He learned quickly. I'm not faulting him. Plenty of people injured in terrible accidents blessed the day Doctor Taylor came to town. Plenty of little ones lived through diphtheria, scarlet fever, measles, and the rest. And, Mrs. Conner did need him when things went wrong."

"Well, I'd die for a trip like that, but I don't envy any of you at that autopsy. I hope I never have to work on a corpse two months dead," Dr. Keller said. "I see the rain has stopped. Perhaps it would be pleasant to finish the day with a stroll through Beacon Hill Park."

Columbia House, Golden, BC. Often attracting crowds in search of dramas and musicals, Columbia House attracted a different crowd in 1899. It became a makeshift courthouse for the first Supreme Court case in Golden, BC.

Doctor Taylor, Golden's only physician. Taylor spent over a month on the trail to exhume the body of Alex McCaulay, and to perform an autopsy.

Judge Tyrwhitt Drake (photo taken 1904). Judge Drake, a prominent member of society from Victoria, tried the case of the Queen vs. James Hughes.

#9 (Fourth man from the left): Thomas O'Brien. The identity of the others is unknown. O'Brien defended James Hughes in the Supreme Court trial of 1899.

The jury for the trial of the Queen vs. James Hughes, and Sheriff Redgrave.

Chapter XIX

The three sat on a bench overlooking James Bay and watched the sailboats gently gliding before the breeze.

"I sometimes think the Cree had more sense than any of us," Percy said. "They bypassed the whole mad scramble. Men, women, and children rode through the mountains to Sullivan River, fished, hunted, picked berries, watched the prospectors pass, and shrugged."

"Yes," Alan said, "They had a more contented life. They were content with what the Lord provided. They also took their families with them, which the white men certainly didn't. The Native families stayed together. But I will admit," Alan continued, "the lure of gold is something hard to resist. If I'd had your chance, I'd have done the same. I've had a good life and I love my family, but still, sometimes I feel that I have missed out on an adventure."

"And sometimes that adventure was ulcer producing," Percy continued. "The more people thought about going north for gold, the more they thought about the dangers, and the more the rumours flew about Alex. Someone heard. . . . a prospector told another who told someone's uncle . . . you know how it goes. It only takes two to start a rumour. They said McCaulay was a wild breed; he robbed men on the trail; left them to starve; went wild when he drank; beat his wife almost to death. They couldn't find enough to say about Alex, and folks believed it.

"When I arrived in Golden to report McCaulay's death, I heard the rumours about the Indian who had attacked Jim Hughes, the prospector. I tried to set the record straight. I said everything I could to prove Alex was a good guy, but people wouldn't believe me. I was amusing, they said, told great stories, but I was a man, and I travelled with that young squaw all the way from Tête Jaune. Of course, I'd say anything she wished."

"Out of curiosity, how did you feel about Adelaide then?" Alan asked. "You say you might have married her."

"Of course I'm a man, always was, but I hope I'm also human," Percy said. "Adelaide had suffered the horrors of Alex's death. She was in shock and mourning. Adelaide was a good woman, and didn't deserve any of what happened. I took her to Golden so she could tell the court. On the trip, I respected her feelings, and kept my feelings to myself. I wanted Hughes to hang for what he did, but when I told the truth, nobody listened. I thought if I took Doc up there he could bring back the evidence, and folks would have to believe him. But that wasn't the way it worked. A lot of things didn't work out the way I'd hoped they would."

As Adelaide rode to the courtroom with Dan, she watched the yellow leaves blow in the wind. She saw new snow that had crept ever further down the mountains. She thought back on the summer, and she was glad the people from home had been with her. She had camped with them, and they had understood about Alex and comforted her. Now, it was time to go back before they were trapped here with their horses.

Dan said he would talk for her at court, and then they would go through the mountains. He would tell the whiteman what she said, then they could go.

Adelaide stayed close to Dan when they were in the courthouse even though Kid, Jack, and the doctor were there. She must depend on Dan here. Soon, the clerk came and spoke to Dan, and they went across into the courtroom.

As she stepped through the door, Adelaide shrunk back. Eyes peered at her from all around, from the back of the room in rows, from the front, from every corner.

Memory flashed. The Canoe Valley! She and Alex going back to their cabin. Evening. Moon shining. Behind them, a wolf howling. Wolves answered from the hills, from every ridge, and from up the river, the answering howls came. Her dog cringed close—so close he trod on her snowshoes. She and Alex rushed forward. Her dog came into the cabin, too.

Adelaide searched the courtroom. Alex had told her about glass windows and glass lamps, and the pictures—people's spirits captured. Long ago, he told her about the beautiful coloured glass at the church, about books and writing at the mission where he went. He did not tell her about the eyes among all these wondrous things—eyes like wolves' eyes in the forest.

Adelaide saw Hughes! She saw Hughes' eyes! She turned to run, but Dan caught her arm. Dan wouldn't let her go.

Hughes was with a man. The man had a gun. Hughes had no gun.

Adelaide looked away. As if Hughes wasn't there, she looked. Adelaide stayed close to Dan. Dan knew about whiteman.

Dan told her the man beside Hughes was like a Redcoat; he was a policeman, and he was guarding Hughes so Hughes couldn't hurt her or anyone. He said the men were here to find out what Hughes did, all except that man, O'Brien. O'Brien would help Hughes.

The spirit of a woman, a white woman, was here. On the wall behind Griffith the spirit of a cranky white woman was captured. No other woman was here, only the cranky spirit and Adelaide. The spirit did not shrink from the eyes.

Griffith spoke, and the clerk took up a book. Dan told her she should put her hand on the book He would say the oath, and she must answer.

In English, she said it, "I so swear."

She told Dan what he already knew, that Hughes shot her man, and her man died. Dan told it to Griffith in English, and Griffith wrote on the paper, and read it. Dan told her what he read.

She took the pen in her hand just like the whiteman did, and she made a cross, upright like the cross on Alex's grave, but small. A cross would represent her signature as she could write no English.

As she put her hand to the paper, the clerk jerked his white hand away as if she was dirty. Adelaide took the pen and made a smaller cross over the lines of the first cross. She made a cross that looked like Jesus there, like the crucifix the priest gave. Maybe the man would like that better. Adelaide put the pen down. The clerk took the pen and made his mark beside her cross.

Dan put his hand on the Bible and swore his oath.

Griffith started to talk. He looked at the paper and he read:

"On the information and complaint of Adelaide McCaulay of Donald, taken this fifth day of September, in the year one thousand eight hundred and ninety nine, before the undersigned, one of Her Majesty's Stipendiary Magistrates in and for the County of North East Kootenay, who saith that James Hughes murdered Alexander McCaulay, on the 12th day of June, 1899, at a camp on the Fraser River, near the mouth of Swift Current Creek, Cariboo District."

"How do you plead?" Griffith asked.

"Not guilty," Hughes said.

Adelaide understood almost nothing. She heard her name, Hughes' name, Alex's name, the Fraser, Swift Current Creek. Those words, she understood. Dan made a sign.

"He did it!" Adelaide cried. "Tell them, Dan! He shot my man!"

"I will tell them." Dan said. "When they ask me, I'll tell them."

Griffith spoke to Dan, but when Dan started to talk, O'Brien said, "Objection! Mr. Noyes is an interested party. He cannot act as interpreter."

Griffith hesitated for a moment, sighed, then answered, "Objection sustained. Court will postpone the evidence of Mrs. McCaulay pending inquiry regarding procuring another interpreter." To the clerk, he said, "Take the witness back, and bring the next witness."

Dan gaped. The clerk beckoned to him, and Dan motioned to Adelaide who followed him from the room. "*Tanehki?*" she implored.

When Kid looked, Dan muttered, "They won't let me talk for her."

Kid blew out his cheeks, "Poof! Who says so?"

"That shit-faced O'Brien."

"And why not?" Kid clamped his jaws.

Dan shrugged. "Maybe I tell the truth," he said.

Adelaide searched Kid's face then Dan's. "*Tanehki?*" she implored.

"I'll tell them," Kid said. "I'll tell them, and Doc will back me up."

Adelaide stood where varnished boards covered the warm earth; varnished walls rose to a varnished ceiling. When she sat, instead of the spruce boughs of their teepee floor, she sat where Kid indicated, on a wooden bench; glass in an ornate frame hung on the wall. A barred window let in the light.

"In a whiteman's place, we can do nothing," she thought. "I want to go back to my own place," she cried.

Chapter XX

"It was about this time of year, September, damn near two months after the folks in Golden first heard of the murder," Percy began, "when Redgrave hauled Hughes out of jail, and Griffith listened to the evidence. That was the preliminary hearing. Jack and I had been out with the Doc for the last month of that time, so I didn't have a chance to defend Alex or to set folks in town straight about the gossip.

"When Hughes went into that courthouse folks knew he'd be charged with murder. They'd heard Hughes had shot some kind of wild man, and they didn't believe he should be charged for that. They knew he'd spent the summer in the coop, and they felt sorry for him. The courtroom wasn't large enough to hold the crowd.

"You should have seen Thomas O'Brien when he entered the courthouse. He was Counsel for the Defence, you know. His first case, and he sure put on the dog. He was a small man, you understand, and cocky as hell. His chin was clean shaven, and his mustache neatly trimmed. His nose didn't add any dignity to his appearance; it was as red as berry wine. He shed his great coat and bowler hat before entering the courtroom. He was decked out in a three-piece blue serge suit, the pants pressed to knife sharp pleats; he had them ankle-high black kid Oxfords spit and polished, celluloid collar, bow tie, and gold cuff-links. His black gown and white tie would be ready for the Supreme Court trial; you could be sure of that.

"But, on that September day, he depended on his gold chain and pocket watch to give him dignity. His cocky manner and the smell of rum that accompanied him across the floor didn't impress me, but I was an exception. Nobody else noticed. O'Brien was the hero of the day.

"Griffith called Adelaide as first witness, and Dan went with her as interpreter.

"O'Brien soon dispensed with him. When Griffith questioned him, Dan said when he crossed the creek, Adelaide was crying. When he asked her what was the matter, she said that Hughes was . . .That was as far as Dan got when O'Brien yelled, 'Objection!'

"Griffith stopped recording Dan's testimony, and considered the objection. Finally, he said, 'Objection sustained.'

"O'Brien had made some kind of objection to the magistrate—that Dan was a friend of Adelaide's—not impartial, you know, and Griffith accepted that. I think they were hand in glove. Years later, I saw the transcripts in the archives, and in the copy he sent to the attorney-general, Griffith didn't even mention about Dan coming as interpreter.

"Adelaide just looked stranded. She had expected to depend on Dan to talk for her, but what could we do? She was sent back to wait for an interpreter. If she'd have got away to her horse, she'd be gone. They wouldn't have found her, ever. As it was, Adelaide and Dan came back to the witness room and sat.

"Doc was the first witness. I was too burned up at the time to notice, but he was a good witness. Everybody liked him and would believe him. Doc was dressed in his best, but even in his best, he looked like a friend from home on Sunday morning. His suit and tie were homespun. His shoes were good practical brogues."

As Doctor Taylor carefully described all of the wounds, Magistrate Griffith recorded his testimony. The doctor closed with the statement that, in his opinion, the wound to the pericardium, the lining of the heart, was the probable cause of death.

Then, Thomas O'Brien began to question the doctor in a suitably gentle manner. His tone sounded sympathetic.

"Have you ever treated a man so wounded?" Mr. O'Brien asked. "May I phrase that differently. In your opinion, would Mr. McCaulay have lived had he received the attention of a physician?"

"I have never come across a man shot in a similar manner," the doctor answered, "Therefore, I am not prepared to say that he would have died even if he had surgical attendance."

"Yes. There was one wound," Dr. Taylor said in answer to another query, "not caused by the bullet. That wound, in itself, would not cause death. The wound in the breast bone was sufficient to cause death."

Mr. O'Brien surveyed his audience.

"Could you describe the wound not caused by the bullet for the jury?" he asked the doctor.

"It was a shallow transverse cut in the abdominal wall. It went no deeper than the skin; there was no connection between it and the abdominal organs," Doctor Taylor answered.

To the next question, Doctor Taylor answered, "The body was too much decomposed; I could not find any marks of probing for the bullet."

O'Brien said he had no more questions, so Magistrate Griffith dismissed the doctor, and called Jack Evans.

Evans had shaved off the beard that had grown during those months in the hills and trimmed his mustache. He wore new clothes, but only what would do service on the trail, a grey shirt and Karss mackinaw pants.

Evans answered straightforwardly and was carefully correct, as if he expected justice would follow honesty. He described the events at Swift Current Creek, as he saw them, and said that he identified the body for Dr. Taylor.

Thomas O'Brien's questions were brief and asked in a respectful manner. "How well," he asked, "did you know Alexander McCaulay? Could you describe his temperament?"

"I first met Alex in March '98 and spent a week with him. I cannot say that I ever saw him angry," Evans answered. To further questioning he answered. "I saw Price make an incision near the naval, a little higher on the right side. It was only skin deep. He did it with an ordinary knife. I couldn't say whether Price administered morphine. Alex could not speak, but he shook hands with me."

Right there, O'Brien said he had no more questions. Griffith dismissed Jack and called for the next witness: Kid Price.

In answer to Magistrate Griffith's questions, Kid told about hearing of the shooting, "When Henry Hollings and Joe Hostyn came for me, they told me Alex had been shot and wanted to see me. I knew Alex well. We wintered together in '97/98 most of the winter. I am in the habit of taking medicine with me into the mountains for emergencies, and Alex knew I could help him. I went over that afternoon, and I found Alex lying on the ground in his teepee. I'd never seen anyone in that condition. The wounds were putrid and crawling.

"As I knelt down by his side and held his hand, Hughes came in and knelt beside me. I looked Hughes in the eye and said, 'I suppose you are responsible for this.'

" 'Yes, I shot him,' Hughes answered. 'Well, you sure as hell did a bad job of it,' I said. Hughes stood up and left. He didn't say a word.

"I had no medicine with me. Everything was at our Swift Current cabin, about three miles away. I sent Jack for the medicine.While he was gone, I did what little I could to comfort him. I examined Alex and found him weak from loss of blood and lack of food. The wounds were in a horrible state.

"After Jack returned, I gave Alex one eighth of a grain of sulphide of morphine, hypodermically. The wounds were fly-blown, and I couldn't remove the maggots, so I applied a poultice of flax seed and left it on till the light of day. Next morning I made a pair of nippers, and using a solution of carbolic acid, 3 parts of acid to 100 parts water, I washed his face. This caused the maggots to move, and I picked them out with the nippers. Alex was in intense pain, so I bathed the wounds with a solution of potash, then with a mild solution of carbolic acid, and poulticed them again.

"Alex complained of the bullet hurting him. He wanted me to cut it out, but I couldn't find it because of the swelling. I put on another flax seed poultice and left it on all day. I hoped it would take away the pain. By nightfall, the swelling had gone down, but I still couldn't locate the lead bullet, so I applied another poultice. The next morning, I could feel the shape of the lead."

Kid straightened in the chair. His voice exhibited a certain pride. "Having no scalpel, I procured a shoe knife which is considered good steel, and after sharpening it, I washed it in a strong solution of permanganate of potash and made a slight incision. Pus poured out of the opening, but bruised flesh and foreign matter remained. Again I poulticed. At noon I removed the poultice and could see the lead. After making the incision a little larger I lifted out the lead."

The lead bullet was exhibited there so Kid pointed to it.

"I extracted the bullet on the 21st, and he died on the night of the 24th."

"How well did you know the man, Alexander McCaulay?" O'Brien began.

"I first met Alex on the 15th of September 1897. I had considerable dealings with him. I may say, also, I was continually with Alex during the time he was sick." Kid eyed O'Brien coldly.

"How much did you probe for the bullet?" A needling tone had crept into O'Brien's voice.

"I did not probe for the bullet."

"You say you used a scalpel to make the incision?"

"I used an old shoe knife."

"I see—an old shoe knife. How then, did you extract the bullet?"

"I used a pair of dentist's forceps. The bullet was barely under the skin."

"How well did you say you knew Alexander McCaulay?"

"During '98, we were most of the time together, being hardly a week apart."

"How would you describe his disposition?"

"I found Alex of a generous disposition, but rather sensitive."

"Oho!" said O'Brien, "A generous disposition but rather sensitive? You didn't find he was a troublemaker?"

"I never had any trouble with him."

"Oh! Is that so? Were you not heard to say that the man who shot McCaulay saved you the trouble of doing so? That McCaulay held up men on the trail?"

Kid's eyes flashed. His jaw tightened. He shouted, "I positively state that I never said that the man who shot Alex saved me the trouble of doing so. I never heard that Alex held up men on the trail, and I swear that I never made any such assertion."

When he was told to sign his testimony, he stepped up and signed with a flourish.

Just as he finished signing, O'Brien asked another question.

Kid spat out his answer: "I did not discuss this case with any witness who has given evidence."

"God! I should have known I couldn't win a pissing contest with a skunk!

Griffith wrote out my statement, and I had to sign it. My hand shook so much nobody could read my signature.

I looked sheepishly at the audience. The lot of us had suffered through Alex's death in an isolated wilderness. When I got to Golden, the shooting was the talk of the town. At the beer parlor, everyone there heard me tell about it. Dan and Jack were there, too, and everybody would remember that.

Finally, Griffith let me go. You should have seen the smug look on O'Brien's face. I was ready to punch his nose down to his boot tops."

"I am surprised that a lawyer was on tap on the frontier," Alan said as Percy paused.

"It just takes a hint of gold to bring the greedy hordes, and lawyers can be hungry," Percy replied. "Hughes got a dandy. Tom O'Brien came from Liverpool. He served his apprenticeship in Canada as private secretary to John Schultz, Lieutenant Governor of Manitoba, no less.

"Schultz had owned a small store in Winnipeg in the early days. He was involved in quelling the Métis rebellion and worked hard trying to get Riel hung long before the Riel Rebellion. He had no love for Métis or Indians either for that matter. Tom O'Brien learned a lot from him.

"When Manitoba became a province they gave the Métis scrip which entitled them to land. Canada didn't survey the land into the river-front lots that suited the Métis life style, so many of the Métis got land far from the river and couldn't see what good it was to them. A lot of Canadian politicians soon became wealthy speculating in Métis scrip, let me tell you, and Schultz was one of them. O'Brien moved from there to Calgary where he worked for a senator. He became an alderman, but the fellows he worked for were making the big money, so he set out on his own and continued on to Golden. He was still under thirty, but he had plenty of experience under his belt when he was admitted to the bar in British Columbia just in time to defend Hughes. Yes, Hughes was well represented in court, but you can be sure it cost him."

"Sounds as if it would," the doctor agreed.

Chapter XXI

When Adelaide entered the courtroom, she looked, again, as if she was facing a pack of wolves. She drew back, ready for flight, but the clerk urged her forward and into the witness box.

Catherine Conner spoke to her, and Adelaide turned to see a woman who dressed like the whites but spoke Cree. Until Adelaide came to the Columbia Valley, she had never seen a white woman. Even in the Columbia Valley, she had never spoken with one.

However, Catherine had spent her life caring for others, and as she spoke, Adelaide sensed some of this. Catherine spoke Cree naturally and well, and Adelaide gathered courage. With the aid of Catherine's translation, Adelaide told her story.

Adelaide described how Hughes followed them from Jasper House because he did not know the way. She told of the repeated quarrels over the saddle and the beaver skins. She told of Hughes threatening to shoot Alex. She told how she and Alex were packing to leave. She graphically described how Hughes shot as Alex saddled the horse, how she ran to Hughes to try to prevent him from shooting again, then ran back to help Alex. She told of Hughes going for Alex's gun, of her helping Alex to the teepee poles.

Adelaide's nervousness visibly increased as she relived her ordeal. Suddenly she cried out, "I wanted the old man to help, but he wouldn't stir." Adelaide searched the audience for a familiar face. She saw a sea of faces, all with expressions that became more avid as Catherine translated.

When O'Brien started his cross-examination, Adelaide answered, "No, the old man did not help me take Alex to the teepee. Alex walked with my help." She answered several more questions.

Suddenly, Thomas O'Brien altered his tone. "Is it not true," he taunted, "That your husband carried a big knife in his belt?"

At the taunt in O'Brien's voice, Adelaide started. She watched O'Brien's mocking smile. She understood a few words.

When Catherine Conner began to translate she listened to the tense voice. "*Mokoman no seguia shu?*" Catherine Conner said.

Adelaide's eyes darted around the courtroom. White male faces leered back at her. When Catherine Conner spoke in Cree, she too, was subjected to the disrespectful stares.

Adelaide turned to O'Brien and flung back her defiance. "*Namoya! Napim mokoman moya miseguit; apsiss!*" And Catherine Conner translated sternly, "No! My husband did not carry a big knife, only a small one," "*Moniyaw moya nesokamen!*" "Whiteman did not help me!"

O'Brien parried and jabbed, "Is it not true that your husband accused you of the shooting?"

"*Namoya!*" Adelaide cried, "My husband did not accuse me."

O'Brien smiled and taunted. Adelaide reacted like an animal trapped. She barked back: "*Namoya!* When Alex and Hughes quarrelled, I did not catch Alex's arm to prevent him from stabbing Hughes.

"I never heard my husband say he would kill Hughes, but I heard Hughes say he would shoot my husband."

She was required to defend Alex regarding the blow she received from his arm immediately after the shooting. "My husband did not beat me. My husband did not hold up men on the trail," she screeched.

Adelaide looked from O'Brien to Griffith, to the sea of faces. The eyes burned her. Mrs. Conner told her there were no more questions. She was free to go, and Adelaide wove her way through the crowded courtroom and out the door.

❖

Thick willows and the steep bank of the Columbia River screened Adelaide from view. She saw Kid scanning the river from above, and she moved into deeper cover. If she followed this river north, she would return to her kinsmen's camp. She could see her horse grazing below.

I left whiteman's court. Where whiteman couldn't find me, I went. I saw Kid looking, but he couldn't find me. I will get my horse, and I will ride. I will go to Sullivan River, and then I will go to Kohkum, go to Kohkum, and Kohkum will braid my hair. She will braid my hair and bathe my feet, and on my feet she will put beaded moccasins. Like I am a little girl, Kohkum will do this.

I told whiteman. I told them Hughes shot my man. Whiteman is crazy. Whiteman said I shot my man. He said my man beat me. He said my man tried to kill Hughes. In front of their cranky spirit I told them. The spirit can be cranky with whiteman, not with me. The spirit can cut off Hughes' thing and feed it to the ravens.

Back to Sullivan River, I will ride. Dan will come, and he will ride that way, too. Now, we can go. Through the mountains, we can go. The people at Sullivan River wait for us.

The people caught many fish. All summer we did this. Kokanee and salmon, we caught, and we smoked them. We tied up the fish. With sinew, we tied. We will put them on the horses, on the pack-saddles. We picked berries, and we dried them, and we put the berries in bags. We made pemmican, and we dried meat, and we will take it, too. All of it we will take through the mountains.

We will ride through the mountains. Before the snow comes, we will ride. When I get back from whiteman's court, the people are ready. We will ride.

Adelaide looked about. Kid had returned to the court, and no one was in sight. With a short whistle, Adelaide called to her horse, and they walked toward each other.

Finally, Magistrate Griffith called for the next witness, Dan Noyes, questioned him, and continued to write as Dan said: "Mrs. McCaulay asked me to go over to see her husband. I went over and saw Hughes standing about ten yards from the teepee. He did not speak to me particularly, but he said, 'Better go in and see the boy. I shot him.'

"I saw Alex lying on the bed of boughs. Alex held out his hand, and I took it, and Alex began to cry. I told him not to cry. I asked him if he knew me, and he said, 'Yes'. I asked Alex if the old man shot him, and he made a sign, yes for two beaver skins.

Alex wanted me to kill the old man for him, but I was scared. I told Alex the Redcoats would look after that."

Then O'Brien began to question Dan, and Dan answered: "I have known Alex for eight or ten years. I lived in the same place with Alex and did a good deal of trading with him. His reputation was good in every way."

Magistrate Griffith wrote: 'I have known McCaulay for eight or ten years. As far as I know McCaulay was straightforward. I have done a good deal of trading with him.'

"You say that Mr. Hughes admitted that he shot McCaulay. Is that so?" O'Brien asked.

"I swear I heard the old man say he shot the boy," Dan answered.

"And, you say that Mr. McCaulay asked you to shoot Mr. Hughes. Is that so?" O'Brien continued.

"He gave signs that lead me to believe he wanted me to kill the old man." Dan replied.

O'Brien said he had no further questions and Magistrate Griffith dismissed Dan.

❖

Adelaide had walked away from the camp, away from Kid and Dan. She felt she has no one with whom she could share her thoughts, so she laid her head on her horse's neck and talked to her horse.

Kid and Dan came from whiteman. They came to the camp. Kid told me I must not go. I must tell the man that comes from the white queen. Another white judge, I must tell.

Whiteman is crazy, I say to Kid. I will go from this place. I will go through the mountains with the people!

Kid said that whiteman with the shiny black boots, the whiteman that said I shot my man, fights for Hughes. Kid said the other whiteman will not believe him. Kid said the whiteman that the queen sends will not believe that whiteman. If I stay and tell him, he will not believe that whiteman. If I go, he will believe the whiteman that fights for Hughes.

Whiteman have a cabin for me, a small cabin. I will stay in the cabin until the judge comes. Whiteman sent food for me. Flour, they brought, and sugar; tea and raisins and prunes, they sent, and bacon, a slab of bacon.

Dan, he stayed. He works for whiteman. He rides into the mountains. When he comes back, he will go to the court. With Kid and me, he will go.

Then, Dan will ride through the mountains with me and Mosie and Mary. Kid, too, he will ride. He will ride with me and the children to Tête Jaune Cache. Dan will go to Henry House. With me, he will go.

My people, they went. They took the fish, and the meat, and the berries, they took. Adelaide's horses, they took. All the horses, they took, except Dan's and my horse, and one pack-horse. Because we must not have too many horses here when winter is coming, they took them. Mary will ride with me, and Mosie will ride with Dan. The rest of the horses, they took, and they rode through the mountains. In the high passes, snow is coming soon. My people must go.

I stay. In the cabin, I stay. Whiteman gave me flour and sugar and tea and raisins and prunes and bacon. All of it, they gave.

Adelaide turned, placed her right hand on her horse's neck and jumped up onto its back. She rode bareback along the trail and around the pasture for a time. Then, desolately, she returned to the camp and joined her sleeping children.

❖

"It must have seemed an endless time to Adelaide, sitting in that witness room not knowing what went on," Percy said to Clara. "Dan had been shut up once, and she didn't know whether either of them would ever be allowed to speak. She didn't know how she could speak without Dan. By the time I got off the stand, I was fuming so much, I walked right out the door, and Adelaide was already on the stand when I had calmed down enough to come back. I didn't stay calm for long. O'Brien was badgering Adelaide. But I will say one thing for Adelaide. She stood up to him.

"I don't know how he did it, but Griffith had found an interpreter, a woman who was some help to Adelaide. Since no one but Mrs. Conner understood what Adelaide had to say, Adelaide had a chance to answer more than the questions that were thrown at her, and Mrs. Conner faithfully translated every word. Small compensation for the way that skunk O'Brien treated her.

"The Cree had spread across Canada, from Quebec to the Rocky Mountains, but not many had penetrated the mountains, and you couldn't have dragged most of those who did into court. If you did, they didn't speak or understood English well enough to interpret. I'm sure O'Brien counted on that to delay the hearing, but as I said, Griffith found an interpreter.

"Mrs. Conner delivered the babies before the doctor came, and Dr. Taylor soon learned to depend on her for help with that. Mrs. Conner had been midwife for ten years, so women knew her. Catherine Conner was like Mama. She knew plenty of home remedies too, and some people still went to her even after the doctor arrived.

"Mrs. Conner and her husband, John, came from St. Boniface, Manitoba, and travelled through the Rocky Mountains on the tote road to Golden during railroad construction days, and stayed for the rest of their lives. On this day in court, Catherine Conner, trim and motherly, wore her good Sunday dress. I'm sure Adelaide feared her at first, but she needn't have.

"When Adelaide was finally able to leave the witness box, she didn't recognize me, or anyone else. She wove her way through the hostile audience and out the door. She looked like she did the day I came to that teepee where Alex lay dying. Moments later when I went outside, Adelaide had disappeared. I looked everywhere for her, but I knew that if she didn't want to be found, I wouldn't find her. Catherine Conner's duties were also completed, and she was free to go. She had come because she was needed, and probably didn't expect pay, but for that horrible day in court, she was paid two dollars.

"Since I couldn't find Adelaide, I decided I'd best go back and see what the hell was happening in that court. As I walked in, Dan was on the stand, and Magistrate Griffith, was questioning him. Dan was as belligerent as a cornered bull moose.

"Dan had never experienced much disrespect. His dad owned the trading post, and among the trappers, that made him a big shot. But here, he had sat in the witness room throughout the hearing, watched Doc, Jack, me, and then Adelaide, leave. Didn't know what was going on. Didn't even know whether he would ever have his say.

"I looked at Dan, and I knew he had no more chance than a snowball in hell. When his dad took him out to the towns, Dan dressed like a white man, but since Alex's death, Dan had been determined to be an Indian.

"Here, he wore the clothes he had on the trail—moccasins, pants and fringed coat, all of moose-hide. The odor of smoked hide in that courtroom was strong. I like that smell, mind, but it sure as hell was out of place in there. The scent of lemon oil, shaving cream, and the whiff of a briar pipe so dear to the gentlemen of the court, all had disappeared. The whole place smelled of smoked hide.

"Dan's accent, his clothes, even his smell was Indian, but his face was white. That was what bothered those gentlemen. They couldn't forgive white blood in an Indian.

"Griffith didn't ask him much, and O'Brien treated him like an idiot. When Dan was asked to sign his testimony, he studied the paper for a long time, then looked puzzled, and signed.

"I've seen Dan's signature. It is a series of artistic curves, beautiful, a work of art. But he hadn't gone to school much, and when he was there, he mostly learned to pray. He hadn't learned enough to understand the words written on that paper.

"Otherwise, Dan was a lot quicker than me to pick up on the fact that O'Brien was twisting what we said. When O'Brien suggested Dan had said Alex asked him to shoot Hughes, Dan corrected him. Dan was careful to say that Alex made signs that meant he should shoot. But it made no difference in the end. The prospective jurors in the audience believed Dan said Alex could speak.

"When Hughes was called to the witness stand. He reserved his testimony for the Supreme Court. You can bet O'Brien had warned Hughes to keep his mouth shut. O'Brien didn't want his client messing up the case. You can bet Thomas O'Brien had told Hughes he preferred to leave the attention where it was."

Chapter XXII

On August 29th, a week before the preliminary hearing, Griffith sat at his desk and calculated the mounting costs.

In two days it would be September; winter was coming. Griffith knew that if the supreme court trial wasn't held soon, it wouldn't be held till next spring. They would have to hold Hughes in the gaol till then.

He turned to his typewriter and wrote to the Attorney-General:

Golden. 29th. August. 1899

Sir,

Reg. v Hughes

Adverting to yours of the 13th, I expect Dr. Taylor back from Tête Jaune Cache tomorrow when Hughes will be tried for murder.

Kindly let me know when the Assizes will be held, and whether it will be necessary to hold Mrs. McCaulay and the other witnesses here in the meantime. Should the trial not come off for some months, Mrs. McCaulay is desirous of going back to Edmonton. This would take considerable time as the distance by trail is in the neighbourhood of Six Hundred Miles.

The two witnesses that went down with Dr. Taylor are trappers on the Fraser River. If they are to remain here, I presume they will have to be paid. If not, they will go back, and we would have to send someone on snowshoes to get them out again, a distance of two hundred miles, altogether. It is going to be a very expensive case, and you will readily see that every effort should be made to have the case come off as soon as possible.

In a few days we will be moving the court house and gaol from Donald to Golden, and we will not be in very good shape to keep prisoners for the next month or two. I would suggest that Hughes be sent to Kamloops or some other place you may decide upon. I shall be glad to get your views on these matters.

> I have the honour to be,
>> Sir.
>> Your Obedient Servant.
>> (signed) J. E. Griffith
>>> Govt. Agent.
> The Deputy Attorney-General
> Victoria.

After the preliminary hearing, Griffith sat and recorded the sums he had paid out. His worries had been well founded; the amount was considerable:

Evans & prospectors, re: trans. accused	$464.10
C. P. Price, for transporting witness	68.72
G.E. McDermott, groceries for Mrs. McCaulay	25.31
Dr. J. N. Taylor, 30 days -	250.00
expenses	17.50
J. W. Evans, 30 days at $2.50	75.00
C. P. Price, 30 days at $2.50 -	75.00
G. E. McDermott, for supplies -	57.30
	$1,032.93

Griffith looked at the total. It did not include the cost of food nor the wage paid Sheriff Redgrave for guarding the prisoner. He knew there were other costs. The expenses already equaled his salary for a year, and the Supreme Court trial still loomed. The Treasurer in Victoria would not be pleased.

Chapter XXIII

A month later, in another small office in Golden, Thomas O'Brien sat and wrote to the Hon. Alexander Henderson, Attorney General of British Columbia:

Golden, B.C. 25th September, 1899
The Honorable,
  Alexander Henderson,
    Attorney-General of British Columbia,
      Victoria, B. C.

Dear Sir:
  Regina -vs.- James Hughes
  Mr. W. C. Wells, M. P., informed me a few days ago that he had a conversation with you in reference to the above matter and that you promised the Government would come to the assistance of the accused in the way of providing counsel and also witnesses for his defence. Griffith, the Government Agent at this point, also notified me to the same effect. I now have a party who knows the Tête Jaune Cache trail and who is willing to go there at an early date, in fact, immediately. His price however is $300. He informs me that he cannot take the trip without having an assistant, and from the enquiries which I have made, I agree that it would be utterly impossible to undertake the trip alone. He further states that he cannot go without having at least $175 as he will have to provide food for the trip for himself, his man, horses, and the parties coming down.

It will also be necessary to obtain the evidence of three or four in Arkansas City where the accused has lived for the past 30 years.

As I understand the Government is under heavy expense in keeping witnesses here, etc. It is absolutely necessary that immediate action be taken, and it has occurred to me that if I were to go to Victoria and discuss the matter with you, some arrangement might be made whereby we could dispense with the expense of sending to Tête Jaune Cache. If you deem it desirable that I should go to Victoria, I shall do so for the sum of $50. The accused is to be tried on the 31st proximo, and it is, therefore, absolutely necessary that no time be lost, as otherwise, his trial will certainly have to be postponed. If you wire me to come, I shall leave here at once.

Awaiting your instructions,

I am, Yours Faithfully,

(Signed) Thos. O'Brien

Thomas O'Brien admired his composition. As he wrote, he had sipped on a glass of whiskey and added dollars to the estimated costs. The Arkansas City suggestion was an absolute inspiration. He could just see Alex Henderson cringing from the dollar signs. Would anyone in Kansas give Hughes, that old reprobate, a character reference? O'Brien thought not. O'Brien knew Hughes' old partner, Bill Cook wouldn't. Would anything in Tête Jaune Cache save Hughes' hide?

I doubt I'll need to find out, O'Brien concluded. He took another sip.

He would arrange for a couple of witnesses. Alan Hampton, he decided, would do.

Hampton was a thief and lied by rote. He would know something about McCaulay, and if anyone asked him if he knew McCaulay's wife he sure wouldn't deny it. According to Hampton, he "knew" every woman in Golden.

Now, O'Brien thought, I need another witness who will repeat the gossip about McCaulay. I want the jury to hear it in court. And I want that moralist, Maclean, to harangue both witnesses. The jury will enjoy that. Thomas O'Brien would have liked good honest evidence to save his client, but, he concluded, a man has to go with what he has.

He sat and mused: the old bugger owned a fine string of horses. No denying that. The horses, together with the saddles and the rest of the gear, tent, bedding, camping equipment and food enough for three months, had fetched a good price, and the old man even produced a few dollars when he was pressed. Then that talk to Wells, money from the attorney-general—not bad for a first case.

Thomas O'Brien imagined the letter arriving in Henderson's office. Thomas had addressed it to Henderson, but Maclean was deputy. He would be the one to deal with it. Even if Henderson got the letter first, he would either make a deal or hand it over to Maclean. Maclean wasn't only deputy attorney-general, he was also a Crown prosecutor. Thomas O'Brien remembered Maclean from Winnipeg. Maclean would be incensed at the offer to make a deal. He would insist on prosecuting this case himself.

Thomas O'Brien looked over at a spider's web. It stretched from the window frame to the filing cabinet. Thomas had watched as the spider spun. Today the web held the skeletal remains of one fly, and Thomas watched as the spider disembowelled another. More flies buzzed around.

Thomas smiled, lifted his drink, acknowledged the spider, drained his glass, and waited.

Chapter XXIV

On the morning of October 30th, the citizens of Golden strolled toward the Canadian Pacific rail station. Men had dressed in Sunday suits. Women wore hats, gloves and fur stoles. Little girls walked decorously on patent leather slippers and tossed their curls at waifs, and their unruly dogs. Little boys with hair plastered down turned the back of their caps to the insults hurled at them by those same waifs. The fathers avoided sardonic glances from loungers.

Mr. William McNeish from Columbia House drove his matched team of grays, silver and brass jingling in tune with the clap of hooves while red trim and black harness danced in time. Buffalo robes on the carriage seats awaited the comfort of dignitaries from afar.

A haunting steam whistle echoed through the mountains, and the assembly listened to clickity-clack, clickity-clack while the engine puffed steam, approached, and passed. The baggage car stood opposite the station when the train stopped.

The baggage man threw off leather luggage, mail bags, and express. The engine steamed and puffed, and the train moved forward till the first class car stopped before the assembled crowd.

The porter stepped off, sat down two Gladstone bags and two brief cases, put down the step, and offered his assistance to Judge Drake. Dressed in great-coat, fur hat, canvas galoshes, a woolen muffler, and woolen gloves, the Judge impatiently declined the offer, climbed down from the car, and planted his cane firmly on the station platform.

Judge Drake with jaw clamped firmly and expression sour, had been on the circuit since early September and had just sentenced a man in Revelstoke to a year for stealing a horse. All through the southern interior, he had tried men for fighting, for trespassing, and for theft. All of them were guilty. He had been heard to say disrespect for the law was everywhere, and he intended to stamp it out. When Mr. McNeish stepped forward with the offer of transportation to the hotel, the judge declined.

"I wish to take my morning stroll," Judge Drake said. "See that my bags are delivered to my room."

After the Judge moved away from the door, the porter offered assistance to Maclean, a younger man than the judge. Maclean politely accepted the offer.

Maclean had come from Victoria but appeared untired by the long journey; he walked firmly and briskly along the platform. He requested that his bags be taken to the hotel, and asked direction to the government office. When there, he introduced himself and asked for Griffith.

To this man from Victoria, the young clerk answered nervously, "I am sorry, Sir. Mr. Griffith has stepped out for the moment. He was not expecting you so soon. Can I be of any help, Sir?"

Maclean inquired whether an interpreter had been located, and the clerk reassured him. Maclean was disturbed to hear that Hollings and Hostyn, witnesses at the first preliminary hearing, were not available.

"They left in July, Sir. I believe they live someplace near Edmonton. They are prospectors, and it would have been very expensive to locate them."

"No, sir," the clerk replied in answer to the next question. "Mr. Cook will not be witness for the defence. He is in Windermere not far away. He knows Mr. Hughes well, but nobody asked for him to be subpoenaed."

"Yes, sir, there are witnesses for the defence, two of them. But I am afraid, sir, one of them isn't an honest man. Well, sir, he stole from the store, and lied about it. And he lives with a woman in a cheap hotel. The woman is not his wife." The clerk lowered his gaze.

"A prostitute?" Maclean asked sternly.

The clerk kept his eyes down. "Yes, sir! I believe that is what they call her."

"Oh yes," the clerk mumbled in answer to the next question. "The other witness is an honest man, I am sure. But he has barely met Hughes and has admitted he doesn't know McCaulay."

"Those are his witnesses? I expected as much," Maclean said. "Mr. O'Brien has been at work." He thanked the clerk for his help and left.

The clerk had noticed that Maclean's expression was very severe. When Mr. O'Brien entered a few minutes later, the young fellow was sifting nervously through some papers.

"What is the matter, boy," Mr. O'Brien said cheerfully.

The youth recounted the exchange he had with Maclean, ending with the words: "Maclean was very angry when he left. He is the head of the government office in Victoria, and I'm afraid I shall be out of a job!"

Mr. O'Brien patted the boy on the back and laughed heartily. "Buck up boy! You did exactly right. Maclean abhors dishonest people. He will be pleased that you have warned him."

❖

Percy's recovery from pneumonia had consumed many dreary months. Clara's and Alan's visit had revived both his keen wit and his penchant for spinning a yarn.

"Judge Drake was an Englishman, descended from a brother to Sir Francis Drake, no less. He came to the colony of British Columbia in '59, and was a prominent, even respected, member of society in Victoria. He'd come to find gold like everyone else, but he wasn't much trained for mucking, so he went back to his practice of law.

"Being British upper crust, he soon became a member of the Legislative Council of Victoria. Of course when Canada began recruiting the colony, Drake was against that," Percy said. "I believe his opinion went something like this."

Percy stood, adopted a haughty pose, and looking down on his sister and nephew, with assumed contempt, spoke patronizingly.

"Confederation may be advantageous to those who are sent as delegates to Ottawa; they would be made men for life, but if it is really so advantageous as we are told, how is it that Newfoundland and Prince Edward Island have not joined the Dominion? I am for representative institutions from top to bottom. If it were possible, I would have the governor elected, but this is impossible. I have been accused of being a Conservative. I deny it entirely. I am an out-and-out radical. I suppose I am pretty near a Republican, but nevertheless I have no desire to see the British constitution infringed upon in any way.'

"Well, Mr. Drake lost out on that argument. I doubt if even the Republicans would have accepted him for long. The Canadians in the colony outnumbered the British, so he exchanged his seat on the legislative assembly and became Mayor of Victoria, that very British city, but in '77 he still hadn't accepted confederation. As mayor, at a dinner to honor a retiring United States consul, he said, 'I looked forward to the day when there would be no need for an American consul in British Columbia.'

"There are more Macs and Mcs in Canada than in all of Scotland, and back then many of those transplanted Scots still spoke Gaelic at home, and still resented the English. The Scots were in a new country, and they had no intention of giving way to English gentry. The Scots were in positions of power in Ontario and the Maritimes, and many of them had migrated west, so when British Columbia joined confederation, the fight was on.

"In Victoria, Drake was elected and served twice as a Member of the Legislative Assembly of the province and became a member of the Board of Education, a position where his opinions were popular in Victoria if not in the rest of the province. His supporters said he loved to ruffle the feelings of the more staid citizens. He loved a good jibe.

"Most Canadians didn't judge him so generously. Those that kowtowed to him soon cooled when he said, 'I thank God I am not a Canadian! I have never met a Canadian gentleman in my life, and if one is to be found it will be in Barnum's museum.' As you can see, Judge Drake didn't win friends. His tactlessness tended to rile a jury. Although he may have desired more respect, this case in Golden was small beans in Judge Drake's career. He sat at the trial when Dunsmuir's kin were fighting over Dunsmuir's will, and his judgment withstood all the appeals even in the highest court of the realm, the Privy Council. That trial lasted for weeks-and the appeals years of time and expense. But, the Dunsmuirs were important people and their case involved important property; it couldn't be handled in a day and a half.

"Hugh Maclean, the prosecutor, should have been received with more favour. He did get some respect from the better citizens of Golden. After all, he was the Deputy Attorney-General of British Columbia, and he was a Canadian Scot from New Brunswick, I think. He was considered a great lawyer—a formidable antagonist. He was Deputy Attorney General in Manitoba before he came west, so I'm sure he and O'Brien had locked horns before, and O'Brien had a way of turning the crowd on a body he didn't like. Maclean was a touch proper for the likings of ordinary folk, so O'Brien had something to work with, and although Maclean scared the hell out of that clerk, the crowd at the trial dismissed him.

"Judge Drake was the big fish. Drake was high society in Victoria, and his outrageous opinions were printed in the Victoria papers. When he came to our little backwater town, everybody took notice. After all, he could fine a man a month's wages, send him to jail, or hang him.

"Those who saw the judge, and you can bet everyone strove for that chance, described him to the smallest detail. Those who heard him speak imitated his every word and gesture. A nose was lifted in the air, a cane swung and planted firmly to aid an arrogant stance. 'I came to this hamlet to hang a man. Hurumph!'

"The Supreme Court *and* high society—in Golden! Folks were in a frenzy."

There was a brisk wind and a touch of frost in the air on that damp October morning. The curious, afoot, on horse back, or with a team and wagon, began their trip to the trial in darkness. Heavy clouds, trapped between the mountains, cast a dark pall over the crowd which had converged on the Columbia House before half-past nine but did nothing to subdue the excitement.

Those with horses had stopped at the public well or at the river to water their horses before finding shelter for the animals at the livery stable or in a friend's barn. Some tethered or hobbled their horses in vacant fields, stripped teams of harness or relieved saddle-horses of saddle and bridle. Others, convincing themselves they would only stop briefly, tied their horses to a hitching rail beside a hotel where they could have a drink before leaving for home.

Two men dressed in mackinaw coats, stagged mackinaw pants, heavy boots, and shapeless hats wove unsteadily down the street from the direction of the seediest hotel in town. As they walked, one of them jerked his thumb and glanced towards one of Golden's citizens. The joker assumed a dignified pose, twirled an imaginary cane, and imitated the gentleman's gait.

"Someone must see that justice be done," he pronounced with proper airs. The fellow fool looked, then winked at his companion and snickered.

"Someone has to carry the lurid details back to Matilda and the boys. Someone has to impress upon them the importance of maintaining a proper life," the wag continued.

The buddy slapped his leg and laughed. "You got it exactly!"

Their eyes fell upon a young woman escorted by a very embarrassed older companion as she picked her way through the crowd. A determined expression added a quaint charm to her innocent face. Her husband determinedly maintained a protective barrier between her and the rough horde.

The two men fell in behind, and while one assumed a mincing pace the other clapped his hand over his mouth suppressing a giggle. The woman unaware of her following, smiled and nodded as she passed a large woman dressed in a heavy sweater buttoned over her heavy breasts. A heavy woolen skirt, a woolen tam, woolen mittens, and boots completed that woman's apparel. The joker imitated the graceful nod but sobered at the glare from that formidable woman.

As they neared the hall, the fool swung around, lifted his hand from an imaginary holster, pointed a stiff finger at a shrub, and "Psing," he said. "Another dead Indian!" The crowd laughed: "Way to go, Dick," one fellow shouted and slapped the joker's back.

The two men paused at the door, straightened themselves, assumed a dignified pose, and entered the hall. The crowd sifted in and drifted toward the seats.

Folks who came from Donald, unless they came a day early, would be late. Even if the train was on time, it wouldn't arrive until after ten. Kid rode from Beavermouth to Sullivan Creek and picked up Dan and Adelaide the day before. They all rode into Golden together.

The hall used for the courtroom at the newly built Columbia House, designed to hold two hundred and seventy-five people, soon filled to capacity.

Prospectors and miners had flooded into town before the winter snows eager for entertainment. Some would stay in Golden for the winter. Some would spend a few weeks in Golden, and then with what money they hadn't spent, pick up their supplies before they returned to their isolated cabins.

Golden, the hub for mining and exploration throughout the Rocky Mountain Trench, had asked their member of the provincial parliament for a railroad along the trench from the American border to the north country. They welcomed the money development brought, but they sometimes despaired at the rough element that accompanied it. Footloose wanderers who had survived a lonely summer in the mountains would form the bulk of the audience at this trial.

Families had attended this hall in the spring for the concert sponsored by the St. Paul's Anglican Church, a festive occasion. The ladies not only attended, but contributed the entertainment. But at this trial, husbands, fathers, and brothers would attend and convey to the women at home such details of the case as were suitable for them to hear.

❖

Percy, in an entertaining mood, picked up one of the yellowed newspapers, pursed his lips, and read in an affected manner:

"The most memorable of these was Miss Devlin who exhibited delicacy of touch and power of expression as she rendered 'The Military Polonaise,' 'The Hunting Song,' and 'Chachoucha Caprice' on the piano. Of the vocalists, the palm was given to Mrs. Robbins who sang 'When Love is Kind' followed by several encores. The Reverend Mr. Munroe sang 'Mary of Argyle,' which was somewhat high for his voice, but his rendition of 'The Holy City,' more suitable to his compass, brought out a well-merited encore of 'Rocked in the Cradle of the Deep.' Mr. Plowright gave a spirited and expressive rendering of 'The King's Highway.' Following these soloists, the Glee Club, consisting of Mrs. Taylor, Mrs. Plowright, Mr. Munroe, and Mr. Plowright sang 'Oh, Hush Thee My Baby.'

Culmination of the evening was the comedy, *Six Cups of Chocolate*, in which six young ladies share their secrets and discover that they have all received identical letters from the same young man."

Percy bowed deeply to his sister as he finished reading.

"Oh! Percy!" Clara burst out. "You're still clowning after all these years. I'm sure the concert was lovely. Much nicer than the terrible things you see on the screen today."

"Yes it was lovely," Percy answered laughing. "That concert took place in the spring of '99, and Golden was starved for entertainment. The Columbia House wasn't prepared for such light entertainment on the last day of October that year."

Percy's mood had suddenly changed, and he launched into a graphic description of the preparations for the trial.

In that makeshift courtroom, the heavy wine-coloured brocade drapes were fastened back at the corners of the stage and the piano was pushed behind one curtain. A large dark walnut desk for Judge Drake occupied centre stage. To the left stood a witness box which had been used as a prop for a play just the winter before. Near the box sat two small desks with chairs, one desk for the prosecutor and the other for the accused and counsel for his defence. A portrait of Queen Victoria flanked by the Royal Crest and the Union Jack graced the back wall, emphasizing the solemnity of the occasion. Below the stage and to the right of the judge's desk, so that they faced both the judge and the witnesses, chairs were arranged for the jury. To the left opposite the jury, a chair for Sheriff Redgrave occupied a space which gave him a view of the court proceedings, the crowd, and anyone who created a disturbance.

Beyond the jury, row on row of chairs filled the remainder of the hall. As people approached their seats, they looked up to four carbide crystal chandeliers which hung from the centre of four moulded plaster flowers. They gazed around at limned oak wainscott and sculptured plaster walls topped by moulded cornices and beading. This portion of Columbia House was completed the year before by a decorator imported from Calgary, and Golden displayed its best to the visiting dignitary.

When Thomas O'Brien walked in and strode over to his chair, there was a murmur of approval. The clerk silenced the audience with a gentle "Quiet please!"

The crowd, still nodding and smiling, watched O'Brien and examined his new black robe.

"He'd look as sharp as any of those swells from Victoria in one of those English wigs," whispered an awestruck voice.

The clerk frowned, and motioned the man to be silent.

"Well, at least, Drake won't be able to hide behind a wig," the same voice whispered, and a laugh rose from the floor.

"Quiet please!" the clerk requested.

Hugh Maclean, the prosecutor, entered, and the crowd eyed him critically as he walked to his desk.

Time passed. People squirmed restlessly. Hugh Maclean and Thomas O'Brien studied papers from their brief-cases. The clerk left through the rear door, and after a delay, re-entered.

"Everyone will please rise!" the clerk prompted, and as the crowd rose to their feet, Judge Drake, seventy years old when he came to Golden that October day, entered and strode toward his desk.

The judge wore a black robe, heavy woolen trousers, a black vest, a white string tie, and as an added vestment, a dour expression. He took his seat, and the crowd shuffled to theirs. That joker, sitting in a front row, touched his hair, then jerked his thumb towards the judge's uncovered bald head.

"Where's his wig," whispered the other buffoon.

"Didn't you know," the joker whispered. "Since the Supreme Court act was passed in Victoria, wearing those English wigs is illegal, even for an English gentleman."

A snicker rose from the crowd. Judge Drake's gavel rose, and he hammered on the desk. "Order in court!" He roared. The crowd obeyed.

The first business of the court in those days was to install a grand jury whose members were chosen from prominent Golden citizens. W. G. Mitchell-Innes, foreman, E. Plowright, W. McNeish, S. G. Robbins, H. Dickson, J. Henderson, S. High, G.H. McDermot, T. Robson, C. H. Parson, J. Dolmage, Thomas McNaught, and J. C. Greene, were all jurymen. Folks in isolated places almost never saw anybody from Victoria. Court was about the only occasion. The grand jury informed the judge about all of Golden's problems which they wished Victoria to correct.

Although the trial only took a day and a half, the grand jury used the first morning of that for apologies and those petitions. They apologized for the courthouse which had been moved from Donald and needed smartening up. That required much explanation. Then, Mitchell-Innes continued to petition the judge. He requested small debt courts in the Kootenay district, police constables without other duties for Golden, Field and Windermere, a lock-up for Windermere, and changes in the method of coroner's inquests. Mitchell-Innes told that Supreme Court Judge every problem in the East Kootenays.

Finally, the grand jury examined the transcripts from the preliminary hearing, found sufficient evidence, and brought in a true bill. The grand jury was dismissed, and James Hughes was charged with murder.

Hughes pleaded not guilty.

The time had come to retire the grand jury and pick the petit jury. They would try Hughes for murder, and they were a different crowd altogether. Twenty-three men were called for jury duty, and O'Brien didn't find reason to challenge many. If the court wanted to find twelve men who hadn't heard all about the shooting in Tête Jaune Cache, they would have had to bring them in on that day's train from a long ways away. They didn't. The picked jury consisted of several prospectors, the local barber, and Joe Stirrett to round out the dozen.

No Indians had been subpoenaed for jury duty.

Chapter XXV

In the court, Judge Drake had disposed of the apologies and petitions of the grand jury and overseen the selection of the petit jury. It was noon. After a break for lunch, the judge prepared to listen to the testimony of the witnesses and of the accused.

In the witness stand, when questioned by Maclean, Dr. Taylor described the course of the bullet, through McCaulay's body, which he said could only be the result of a shot fired from above, or when McCaulay was in a stooped or prone position. He described the wounds from the bullet saying that the chest wound, where it pierced the lining of the heart, was very serious and the probable cause of death.

"I examined his body," the doctor said, "and found nothing else to explain his death. It took the whole afternoon to make the examination," he said.

Maclean had finished his questioning, and O'Brien rose to the floor to cross-examine Dr. Taylor. "I hear from your testimony that the wound, coming as it did, so close to the heart was a very serious problem. Were there after-effects of that wound? Did it cause any infection?"

"Yes. There was pericarditis, a very serious infection around the heart," the doctor answered.

"I see. Pericarditis. I believe that is a very serious condition, indeed. Would you say, he might have lived if he was in a hospital, if he had professional attention?"

"Possibly, he could have lived if he had medical treatment," Dr. Taylor admitted.

"I believe the abdomen is an unprotected and very sensitive area. Could a blow there, or a cut, cause death?"

"Yes," the doctor agreed, "A blow in the stomach or a cut there could cause death."

"And the cut in the abdomen, was there danger that it, too, especially under such primitive conditions, could, as did the wound near the heart, become infected?" O'Brien spoke quietly, respectfully.

"Yes! There was danger of blood poisoning from the cut in the abdomen," the doctor admitted.

"Would there be anything, under the conditions in the teepee, that would increase the danger of blood poisoning?" O'Brien continued.

"Yes," the doctor answered. "In the heat of summer flies gather. Maggots from fly blows increase the liability of blood poisoning."

"That is all for the moment," Mr. O'Brien said to the doctor then nodded significantly to the jury.

❖

Dr. Keller had listened to Percy recount Dr. Taylor's testimony. "The only advantage a hospital would have had over your location was that the patient, especially with a young doctor like Dr. Taylor, would have received aseptic treatment rather than the antiseptic treatment on which you had to rely," he said. "The doctor would have boiled his instruments for twenty minutes. He would have scrubbed his hands and donned a cap, gown, and gloves. He would have depended on extreme cleanliness instead of carbolic acid, and he would have used fomentation instead of poultices.

"However, the wound in the patient's abdomen was already septic when you arrived, and he had developed pericarditis. Possibly a doctor could have given him nourishment and fluids that would help his body heal itself. That was impossible for you. Nevertheless, that was before the development of antibiotics. He most certainly would have died! At any rate, the man was far from a hospital when the fool shot him. That in itself should have brought a conviction. He couldn't have possibly lived through a trip over that trail."

"The remark about the blow or a cut on the stomach was a lawyer's trick," Dr. Keller continued. "Of course, a blow on the stomach will kill if it is hard enough and the recipient is unprepared. The bullet was the most severe blow the patient received. A cut on the stomach will kill if it is deep enough or if bacteria is introduced. In this case, the cut was not deep, and the bacteria was already there." As Dr. Keller talked his impatience with court justice rose.

"I knew Alex couldn't recover, and so did Doc, but we were in court," Percy explained. "We knew we were being tricked, but all we could do was answer the questions."

"It was up to the prosecution to put the right questions to you. He had no right to expect the jury to see through the defence's strategy. He surely suspected that they didn't want to see the truth, and it was up to him to spell it out to them." Dr. Keller continued to speak heatedly in defence of his uncle.

"Whatever the reason, we never did get a chance to state our case," Percy answered.

"You couldn't have known at the time, nor could the doctor," Dr. Keller continued more calmly, "but rather than causing septicaemia, or blood poisoning as they called it, maggots clean a wound. Maggots consume only dead flesh. The doctors at the front discovered that during the First Great War."

"Yes," Percy replied, "I wish I had known that. But you can hardly blame us for thinking the maggots were bad. Maggot-infected wounds sure stunk. We called it the smell of death."

Percy and Alan had been sitting in the lounge of the residence waiting for Clara who was visiting with one of the women. Now, as Clara joined them, they rose to leave. They had planned an excursion to Vancouver aboard the *Princess Elizabeth*.

❖

The clerk had escorted Dr. Taylor back to the witness room and returned with Dan Noyes. He escorted him to the witness stand and took his oath. Hugh Maclean began to question Dan.

"I live in Edmonton." Dan looked warily at Maclean and dropped his eyes as he answered.

"Could you explain to the jury what brought you to Swift Current Creek?" Maclean looked directly at Dan, looking into his eyes whenever Dan looked up. Maclean's voice was gentle and encouraging.

"Last spring I started to go to Swift Current Creek. I started in March, late in March. Some men were going, and I would help with the horses."

"I have a map here," Maclean prompted. "Could you show the jury the route from Edmonton?"

"We started here and followed the trail over to the Athabaska River. Me, and Hollings, and Hostyn, we went up the Athabaska River to here. Sam Derr and Bill Cook joined us there. We stayed around for a while because the snow was too deep. In the mountains, the snow was too deep for the horses to paw for grass. We went through the Yellowhead Pass. Past Moose Lake we went, to Swift Current Creek. Swift Current Creek joins the Fraser River here, near Mount Robson. Tête Jaune Cache, it is here, further down the river."

As Dan traced the map, he gradually relaxed and appeared confident.

"Did you know the prisoner before you met him at Swift Current Creek?" Maclean asked.

"No! I never knew him. I never met him."

"Did you know Mrs. McCaulay?"

"Yes! I knew Mrs. McCaulay. I knew her before I saw her at Swift Current."

"Where and when did you see her at Swift Current?"

"She was at the crossing, where we cross with the horses. I think I met her on June 18th. She came to the opposite side. She waved to us to come over. It was about three or four o'clock when she came."

"What did you do then?"

"I went over. She was crying very much. 'Alex is shot,' she said, and she tugged at me and pulled me towards the tents. Hughes was standing in front of his tent with his hands in his pockets. The men followed us over, and some of them shook hands with him. He said, 'You better go in and see McCaulay. I shot him.'

I ran to the teepee. McCaulay was in bed. His face was all torn up. His right eye was torn out. His chin and his jaw were torn to pieces. He had a wound in his chest. He tried to tell me his condition."

"How did he tell you?" Maclean looked skeptical.

"He spoke in Cree. I could not understand everything. He made me to understand that he was going to die."

"I said, 'No!' I said, 'You will pull through.'"

"He said, 'No!' He pointed up. He said he had been shot for nothing. He pointed to the beaver skins and held up two fingers. He pointed to Hughes tent. There was a scratch on his right hand. He tried to explain that the bone of his jaw had struck his hand. He did this with signs."

"For two beaver skins he was shot!" Dan pressed his words out through clenched teeth.

"What did you do? Could you do anything for him?" Maclean asked.

"I stayed with him for six days. Until he died, I stayed. I buried him."

"Did you know Alex McCaulay for a long time?"

"For eight years, I knew him. Maybe for ten years. I lived in the same place with him."

"What kind of a man was he?" Maclean asked.

"He was a good man. His reputation was good in every way."

Maclean noted his answers: have known him for eight or ten years. Lived in the same place with him. His reputation good in every way.

"What was McCaulay's condition when you saw him in the teepee?" Maclean asked.

"Alex was suffering very much."

"And what was his condition when you knew him before that?"

"He was always in good health, healthy always."

"Would you describe for the jury how big of a man the deceased was. How old he was."

"Alex was only twenty-nine years old. He was thin, not so big as Hughes."

"That will be all," Maclean said. "I believe Mr. O'Brien wishes to ask you a few questions."

Mr. O'Brien rose and walked over to the witness box crowding in close to Dan.

"Would you please tell the jury what you saw when you got to Swift Current Creek?" Mr. O'Brien began.

"I saw a tent and a teepee," Dan replied.

"And people? Did you see people?" O'Brien prompted Dan in an exasperated tone.

"First I saw Mrs. McCaulay, and then I saw Alex and the two children. They stayed in the teepee. I saw the prisoner near the teepee."

"You say you talked to McCaulay, and McCaulay talked to you. Is that right?"

"Price and I talked to McCaulay a lot. We tried to cheer him up. We had little jokes."

"And what did McCaulay talk about?"

"He said to me, 'Go out and kill the old man.'"

"And what did you say to that?"

"I said, No! The authorities will look after that."

"And then, were there more jokes?"

"No jokes took place after he said he was going to die."

"How long did you know Mr. McCaulay?"

"I knew him for eight or ten years."

"Where was his home?"

"He lived at Henry House."

"Where is Henry House?"

"It is about two hundred miles from Edmonton, southwest from there."

"And you say you live in Edmonton?"

"Yes!"

"That will be all. I have no more questions of the witness, Your Honour."

Dan wandered down into the audience, and looking around, he saw no empty seats, so he wandered out the door. He wandered on down the street, muttering, "I spent the whole damn summer here. I was waiting for the trial. I was going to tell them damn whitemen. What did I tell them. Nothing!" He continued aimlessly down the street.

In the courtroom, Jack Evans took the stand.

"When and where did you first meet Alexander McCaulay?" Maclean asked.

"I had been in the upper country since '97. I met McCaulay in Price's cabin at the mouth of Camp Creek in '98."

"When was the next occasion that you met him?"

"On June 19th, '99, after the shooting."

"Please tell the jury where you were on the morning of June 19th.

"I was at my camp at Starvation Flats."

"Would you describe the location of that camp to the jury?"

"Starvation Flats is on the trail about eight miles south of Tête Jaune Cache. It is on the McLennan River."

"Were you alone at that camp?"

"Mr. Price was with me."

"What happened on that day?

"Price and I were working in our garden. About one o'clock in the afternoon, Hostyn and Holland came and told us McCaulay had been shot. We caught our horses and started for Swift Current Creek which was a distance of about twenty miles."

"Would you describe the community of Tête Jaune Cache for the jury. Did you pass any homes on the way?"

"No! There was no one on the trail. No one lives at Tête Jaune Cache."

"When did you arrive at Swift Current Creek?"

"We got to Swift Current about eight in the evening."

"And what did you do then?"

"Price went to McCaulay's teepee, and I went to the camp of the Edmonton men. After supper, I went to the teepee, and Price asked me to go to the cabin. We have a winter cabin three miles up Swift Current, and I went there and got some medicine. I got back to the teepee about eleven."

"Who was at the teepee when you returned?"

"Price was there, and Mrs. McCaulay, and I think, Dan Noyes. Alex McCaulay was there. He was very low. The wounds were putrefied."

"Would you describe the wounds for the jury?"

Jack Evans gave a detailed description of the wounds which confirmed the testimony of both the doctor and Dan Noyes. He finished with the statement, ". . . the ball finally lodged in his abdomen."

"How long did you stay in the teepee that night."

"I stayed for about two hours. Then I went to bed."

"What happened the next morning?"

"I went to see Price and I discussed what to do. Hughes had gone to the camp of the Edmonton men, and while he was away from his tent, we went and took the rifles, a Remington and a Winchester. There were no cartridges in either. The cartridges were at the head of the bed."

"What did you do with the rifles?"

"I took the rifles into McCaulay's teepee. The Winchester, I was told, was McCaulay's. The other I kept. This is it." Jack identified the rifle among the exhibits.

"Would you describe the rifle for the jury?"

"It is a .45-.90, a heavy rifle, sighted at a thousand yards. It takes a .45-calibre shell."

"Were there any provisions in the tent?

"I saw about 150 pounds of flour, bacon, beans, tea and coffee, dried fruit, and some canned stuff, about three months supply of food."

"And in the teepee, was there food?"

"Mrs. McCaulay had some flour, a little tea, and dry beaver meat."

"What did you do after you confiscated the rifles?"

"I hid Hughes' rifle, and then I talked to Hughes. He asked me what I would do in his position. I suggested he should turn himself in, and he agreed to come with me to Donald."

"After he agreed to come to Donald, what did you do?"

"I took measurements and made a diagram which I gave to Mr. Stirrett. McCaulay had a teepee. Hughes had a square tent with the door in the end away from the teepee. There was about twenty yards between them. Mrs. McCaulay pointed out the spot where the horses stood at time of shooting. I paced from where McCaulay's gun lay at his teepee to where he was shot. The distance was forty feet. From where McCaulay was shot to the tent door where Hughes was when he shot was 65 feet."

"What did you do next?"

"I went up to our winter camp for supplies. Mrs. McCaulay was very short of food. After I came back, I prepared to take Hughes to Donald."

"Did you and Mr. Hughes travel alone?"

"No! There was Sam Derr, Holland, Hostyn, Hughes and myself. I brought out Hughes' gun, McCaulay's shirt, and McCaulay's hat with a hole in the brim."

"Thank you. That will be all." Maclean turned to Mr. O'Brien. "Your witness," he said.

"Was Mr. McCaulay living when you left for Donald?" Mr. O'Brien asked.

"Yes, Mr. McCaulay was alive when I left."

"Did you see McCaulay again after that?"

"I returned to Swift Current with Dr. Taylor. We arrived on August 16th, and I exhumed the body and identified it as that of Alex McCaulay."

"Were you present at the post mortem?

"Yes."

"Did Dr. Taylor extract the bullet?"

"No. He did not find a bullet."

"Did you see anyone extract a bullet while McCaulay was alive?"

"The bullet was not extracted when I left."

"Would you describe the prisoner's outfit for the jury?" Mr. O'Brien continued.

"Mr. Hughes had a very good outfit. He had horses, gear, provisions. Everything necessary for a summer's trip."

"And how did the prisoner behave when you suggested he should come to Donald?"

"He gave us no trouble. He agreed to come."

"On the trip, was he troublesome there?"

"He behaved very well on the trip. He gave us no trouble."

The jury and the audience nodded in agreement.

"No more questions," Mr. O'Brien said.

The next witness called was Kid Price. As he left his seat, he looked at Adelaide and nodded.

As Maclean questioned him, Kid began. "On June 19th, I was at Starvation Camp, ten miles south of Tête Jaune Cache. Because of what the men told me, I went that day to Swift Current."

"Did you know McCaulay?" Maclean asked.

"I had known McCaulay quite well. I lived very much with him the winter of '97/98."

"Would you describe the man, his age and appearance, to the jury?"

"McCaulay was 28 years old, of a very light build, about 140 pounds."

"Please continue. Tell the jury what you saw at the teepee."

"I got there at sundown. McCaulay took my hand and put it on his heart and cried. One eye was shot away. Noyes was there. McCaulay could say some Cree, and Noyes could understand him by his signs and certain words. He said he was all torn to pieces and he was going to die." Kid continued to describe Alex's condition his voice thickened and he had to keep clearing his throat.

The judge wrote: Witness describes wounds.

"What did you do then? What treatment did you give?"

Kid continued: "I had medicine at Swift Current Camp three miles up stream. Evans went for it, and when he came back, I gave McCaulay a hypodermic injection of morphine and put a poultice on. Next thing I washed the wounds with carbolic acid and water.

I could do little with his breast wound. The bullet was in his abdomen. I found maggots in his face. I washed the wounds and removed the maggots. I poulticed the wounds and found a swelling on his abdomen which I poulticed. I also gave him an injection on the 21st. I found the swelling down and found I could feel the bullet. I made an incision over the bullet, removed it, and put another poultice over the incision."

Maclean wrote: Extracted bullet. Treatment of wounds.

Kid identified one of the exhibits and continued: "This is the bullet. He got weaker and weaker from lack of nourishment. I tried to feed him with a funnel, but, I could not. He died on June 24th, and we buried him on the evening of the 25th.

"Subsequently I returned with Dr. Taylor and exhumed the body, and Dr. Taylor held a post mortem. On the night of the 21st, the prisoner came into the teepee," Kid continued.

"Objection!" O'Brien called. "Witness was a constable, and took prisoner under arrest."

"Objection over-ruled," Judge Drake pronounced. "There is no evidence that Mr. Price was a constable or that he arrested prisoner."

"I said to Hughes, I suppose you are the person responsible for this? He said, 'Yes! I shot him.' Although I stayed there until the next morning, I was uneasy. He had both guns. I kept watch on Hughes' tent until morning, and then I spoke to him and tried to find out the trouble. I asked him why he would shoot that man down in the presence of his wife and family so far from civilization. He said McCaulay was taking all the provisions and furs, they had a quarrel the day before, and McCaulay would leave nothing for him to get out of the country. Hughes said, had McCaulay given him grub to get away, he would have left him unmolested. If he did not, he would kill him. Hughes said,

'McCaulay was packing up the things and it made me very mad, and I thought he had his gun lying near while he was packing the horse. I took up my gun and shot.'

"When I went with Evans into the tent to get the guns, we found that Hughes had all the grub. The McCaulays had almost no food," Kid continued.

"No more questions, Your Honour," Maclean said turning to the judge.

Mr. O'Brien stood and looked contemptuously at Kid. "You seem to remember minute details of events and conversations. Did you, in fact, take notes?"

"No! I did not. I have given the sense and the meaning of the conversation."

"I see! And you say that McCaulay spoke to you. What did he say?"

"He said he expected to die, and then he would cheer up."

"I see! Was this all he said to you?"

"McCaulay tried to talk a good deal."

"I see! And what language did he speak?"

"He spoke chiefly in Cree."

"I see! And you understand Cree?"

"I understand a little. He tried to explain in English. We had to use signs."

"I see! How long have you been in Canada?"

"I came to Canada fifteen years ago."

Members of the jury looked at each other and nodded.

"I see!" said O'Brien, "And where did you live before that?"

"I was born in the United States."

"Perhaps you can explain to the jury why you left the States."

"I left Idaho to better my condition."

Someone in the jury snickered.

❖

"All morning and into the afternoon, we sat in that damn witness room. I rolled one cigarette after the other. Jack and Doc sucked on their pipes, and the two witnesses for Hughes puffed on cigars and eyed Adelaide. Adelaide sat. She was accustomed to a smoky teepee, so I don't think it was the smoke was bothering her. She had vented her anger after the hearing, but hadn't mentioned that experience since. Nonetheless, she hadn't forgotten."

Clara and Alan had joined Percy at the residence, and they sat silently sipping tea while Percy continued to recount his experiences so many years past.

"When Adelaide and Dan whispered to each other in Cree," Percy continued, "a court attendant stepped forward. 'English please!' He scolded. Dan gestured to Adelaide and they both stopped talking.

"If you didn't know her, Adelaide looked calm, but I knew her mind was in turmoil. She remembered O'Brien with dread and fury. Everything told her she was a prisoner in the whiteman's world. Her bottom must have ached from the hard wooden chair and her back from sitting like a white woman. How much hope did she have that Hughes would be punished by white men? Jack and I talked, but Adelaide and Dan sat for hours without saying a word. I saw Dan gesture to Adelaide, and I nodded trying to encourage them. Adelaide dropped her eyes.

"I had expected to see Mrs. Conner as interpreter, but no such luck. When I walked into that courtroom and saw Archdeacon McKay, I just groaned and slumped down into a seat. In the courtroom that day, in his heart of hearts, do you think he remembered his own native blood? Do you think he sympathized with the trapper and his family? I'll tell you.

"McKay worked alongside the police in the Riel Rebellion. I'd heard him admire Almighty Voice, the Cree who was outlawed because he had a disagreement with the clergy. The church didn't approve of the way he collected women like a housewife collects bits of string. When the police went after him, Almighty Voice shot one of them, so he really was in trouble.

"McKay ended that story with the boast that his brother, James, lead the posse that shot Almighty Voice. I don't know whether it was a reward for that deed, but James later became a Supreme Court Judge. The Archdeacon's father was the Hudson Bay factor, and raised a family of achievers.

"At a fancy dinner the Archdeacon bragged that, at his graduation from Cambridge, the hall resounded with cheers at the announcement that McKay would carry the Gospel of peace and love to the ignorant and bloodthirsty red man. Actually he graduated from St. John's College in Winnipeg, but that's another story.

"Poor Adelaide! She needed a sympathetic ear, someone who could speak her language. She got George McKay.

"For his one day in court, the archdeacon was paid thirty dollars. That is rather more than the two dollars Catherine Conner received for interpreting at the preliminary hearing."

Percy paused and peered out the window. "What do you know?" he said. "The day is nearly over. I must have talked for hours. Would you like to take a walk around the grounds before the sun sets? It would be refreshing."

Chapter XXVI

A delaide sat in a whiteman's building. Only she and the crazy men had not gone into the courtroom. She sat, alone, afraid, and angry. Kid and Dan had said that the judge and the counsel who came on the train would make the people obey the law. Hughes murdered Alex. Hughes would hang, they said. She looked around and saw the crazy men staring at her greedily.

This is whiteman's world, but I will tell them, she thought.

Kid came back, and he was angry. She could see that he was angry. They didn't let him tell; the judge off the train didn't help him, she thought.

When the clerk beckoned, she hesitantly followed him through the courtroom door. From the roof above on a shining chain, glittering ice hung ready to stab her. The spirit of ice hung ready to stab. From the spirit world, eyes followed her wherever she moved. She could feel her long black skirt fold and unfold around her ankles as she walked. The dark blanket around her shoulders could not hide her. Her moccasins glided silently while footfalls around her echoed on the hardwood floor. Chairs scraped. Here, no birds sang. No leaves rustled. No water murmured as it flowed. She smelled white men, the sweet smell of their soaps, the acrid smells from their bodies, tobacco, beer, and smells she did not know. The air stung her nostrils. English voices echoed from the walls.

Adelaide saw another Métis. He was a little bit Cree, not much. His collar told her he was a priest. Like a Catholic priest, but his dress was different. Adelaide watched him put his hand on the book and speak to the judge. Then to her, he spoke in Cree.

He spoke Cree well. He had learned Cree when he was little, not like the priests who learned some to tell the people they should come to mass and bring their children. She looked at his eyes, but he looked away. He could tell what she knew, and he was angry because she knew. He wants to be a whiteman now, she thought. Adelaide put her hand on the book just the way he told her. She felt frightened, but she said it in Cree. She said what he told her to say in Cree. The priest told her he would tell them what she said. She could speak in Cree.

Another man began to talk, and the priest told her. What he asked, the priest told her. She answered what he wanted, and the priest said it in English.

"I am widow of the deceased."

"Do you have children?"

"Three children, two living, a boy and a girl, I have."

"How old was your husband?"

"My man had thirty summers."

"Husband about thirty," the Archdeacon said.

"Do you know this man?" Maclean asked pointing to the prisoner.

"I know the old man."

"When and where did you first meet him?"

"I saw him the first time last winter at Buffalo Prairie."

"And where is Buffalo Prairie?"

"A day's ride south of Henry House, is Buffalo Prairie there."

"Were you at Henry House?"

"I lived with my man last winter at Henry House."

"And when did you go to Swift Current Creek?"

"In spring we came to that place."

"Who went with you to Swift Current Creek?"

"Two children, my man, and the old man, we came."

"Why did you go to Swift Current Creek?"

"The old man, he was going. He said gold was there. He asked McCaulay to take him. We waited for the old man for three days. We met him on the way."

Adelaide stood straight and tall. She had waited the whole summer. She would tell her story.

In answer to the questions she said, "My man traded for a sack of flour at Moose River. He cached half of it. For when we go back, he cached it. We travelled three days, and he killed a bear. After travelling for two days, my man killed two beaver in his traps. Next day, we found the old man's horses had gone away, and my man told him about it.

"The old man went for the horses. When he came back, McCaulay said to him, 'Did you find your horses.' The old man said, 'My horses aren't lost.' The men got angry, and I went away to make bannock and tea. The old man went in the tent, and he ate there. My man went and found his horses, and the old man found his also.

"At Swift Current, my man went up and down the creek to trap beaver. The men did not speak because of the fight about the horses. They made friends again, and they went trapping, both of them to set the traps. They went to Tête Jaune; the next day, they went, and they met two men. The two men came to Swift Current with them, and they talked to them. After that, they were friends. Alex and Jim were friends. They went to the traps, and they brought in six beaver. Three days after, they went again and brought in one beaver. I fixed the skins. We would go back to Henry House, and the old man, he would stay at Swift Current. The day before we would go, the two men were angry again. In the teepee, they were angry. Before that, the old man gave my man a saddle. The old man said, 'I didn't give you that saddle.' The two men started to swear at each other. The old man said, 'Alex, I will kill you!' And my man said, 'Kill me at once.' "

"Did either of them have a weapon?" Maclean asked.

"No! Neither had a gun. Very early in the morning, my man went for the horses. While he was gone, the old man came over, and he asked for beaver skins. I said, 'I don't know.' My man brought the horses, and the old man asked for beaver skins. My man said, 'Which beaver skins? Did you kill any?' The old man turned, and he went into his tent. I then helped my man to pack the horses. My man was packing the last horse. I held. The old man shot my man."

"Did you see the prisoner aim the rifle at your husband?" Maclean asked.

"No! I did not see the old man point the gun at my man. I heard the bang, and I saw the smoke over by the old man. The old man was standing by his tent with his gun. He was working at the gun. The horse jumped, and my man fell. I ran to the old man, and I said, 'Why have you done this?' The old man swore at me, and he motioned me to go away. I ran back to my man. I saw the old man go to the teepee and take my husband's gun. It was lying on the ground. The old man pulled the gun cover off."

As Maclean fired questions at her, she continued to answer.

"No! My man had a knife in his belt, none in his hand."

"My man had his hat over his eyes, and he stooped to get the cinch."

Adelaide pointed to her husband's hat on display. "This is my man's hat. See the bullet hole. This is my man's shirt. See there! That is my man's blood all over the shirt."

Adelaide stared angrily at the jury. Then, she dropped her face and cried.

Maclean paused for a while allowing Adelaide time to compose herself. The court was quiet. "Before you heard the rifle, was there a hole in your husband's hat?" Maclean continued.

"No! There was no hole in my man's hat before the old man shot it there."

Archdeacon McKay interpreted, "I did not see the hole before the report of the rifle."

Judge Drake grimaced and scribbled a notation, "Na moya—no."

"What did you see after you heard the report of the rifle?"

"My man was sitting up. His hat was over on the ground. There was a hole in his face where his eye was before." Adelaide continued wildly describing the wounds.

"What happened when the prisoner went to the teepee?"

"My children screamed and screamed.

"My man tried to get up. He pointed to the children and to me. He motioned to the old man not to hurt us. He held out his hand to the old man to tell him he wouldn't fight any more. The old man came, and he shook my man's hand. Then, he turned and went to the teepee and threw down a blanket for my man. He went to his tent then.

"My man tried to help, and I helped too, and we went to the teepee, and my man laid down there. For two days the old man walked one way, and he walked back. He did not come into the teepee. He walked near the teepee, and he walked away. For two days and two nights I tried to fix my man, to help him. Then, when the old man came near the teepee, I went and pushed him there to show him my man was dying. He sat down by my man and talked to him. My man tried to talk but the old man couldn't understand. After that, the old man chopped wood for us and he brought water.

"He dug a grave, but there was water in it. He dug another, water in it. He said he could not pack the boy to where there was no water.

"Yes! My man was alive then. He knew the old man was digging a grave. He could hear the old man digging."

Adelaide told of caring for Alex for five days until the first men, Dan Noyes and the others with him, came, followed by Evans and Price.

"The old man had grub in his tent. He had bacon, flour, beans, tea, prunes, raisins, many things. He did not give us any. In the teepee we had beaver meat and a little bit of flour. We had no tea."

Archdeacon McKay spoke to Adelaide in Cree, and while Adelaide answered, Judge Drake doodled in the margin of his bench book. He drew a louse with all its crawling legs. He drew a plant with leaves and a blossom.

Maclean turned to the judge. No more questions he said.

Mr. O'Brien rose and began to cross-examine Adelaide.

"Do you speak or understand English?" he asked.

"I don't talk English. Some, I understand."

"Was your husband younger than the prisoner."

"The old man was a bigger man than my man."

"Did the prisoner set traps and catch beaver?"

"The old man had one large trap and two small; he caught one small beaver."

"This old man, you seem to have watched him. You saw everything he did right from the day you met him. Why did you look at him all the time?" O'Brien turned and winked at the jury.

Seeing this, Judge Drake drew a snake coiled and ready to strike.

"I watched him as I was in dread of him," Adelaide answered the last question.

"You say the prisoner gave your husband a saddle. Did not your husband owe the prisoner beaver skins for that saddle?"

"My man returned the saddle the day of the quarrel."

"I believe you said your husband shook hands with the prisoner after the prisoner had shot him. Is that right?"

"Yes! My man shook hands with the old man."

O'Brien looked at the jury, raised his eyebrows, and then turned back to Adelaide. "I believe you said your husband talked to you after he was shot. Is that so?" he asked.

"My man spoke to me in Cree after he was shot."

O'Brien asked no more. Archdeacon McKay told Adelaide she could go where she pleased. The Crown's case was closed.

Adelaide wandered down past the crowd. No one made a place for her to sit, so she wandered out of the door. She didn't know whether McKay told them everything she said. She doubted that he did. She went to find her horse. She would get her children. She would go back to Sullivan River. When she went to get her children, Mrs. Conner told her she shouldn't go away. She should wait and see what happened in the court.

Chapter XXVII

James Hughes entered the courtroom shortly before noon, and Judge Drake watched him sit through the jury selection alternately nervous and confident. When the jury was complete, he appeared confident. He should be. Judge Drake looked the jury over—a rough looking lot. Most of them would shoot an Indian for sport, the judge concluded.

Judge Drake had watched the prisoner's reactions throughout the day. As Maclean examined the witnesses, Hughes seemed to be set adrift, but when Thomas O'Brien questioned them, Hughes acted as if he had snagged a life raft. He clung for life to every word.

The judge speculated over how O'Brien had won that faith. First, he laid on the guilt. The judge had no doubt of that. The old fool wouldn't have considered himself guilty. O'Brien would have pointed out to him how the law worked, and then, O'Brien would take everything the old chap owned.

Judge Drake imagined O'Brien squeezing the last penny out of the man. Hughes' outfit should have been enough. During the rush for gold, men would die for that, but the judge wondered what else O'Brien got—probably a retainer from the Attorney-General's office.

As Adelaide left, Judge Drake looked sourly at Hughes. Judge Drake's back ached and his right hand cramped constantly. He wished he could hang the man and get it over with. His bladder was ready to burst.

"The prisoner will take the stand," the Judge said. Hughes rose and walked to the witness box. When he was duly installed, the Judge asked, "What is your name?"

"James Hughes."

"Do you, James Hughes, swear to tell the truth, the whole truth, and nothing but the truth, so help you God?"

"I so swear."

"Your age is?"

"I am 57 years old."

"And what is your place of residence?"

"I lived last winter on the Athabasca River. Before that I lived in Arkansas City."

"Do you have a family?"

Hughes nodded. "I have a wife and five children living," he murmured.

"You might have thought of that family before you acted in such a thoughtless manner," Judge Drake pronounced. He noticed just the suggestion of a tear in the prisoner's eye. Crocodile! the Judge thought. Someone in the jury gave a sympathetic sigh. Judge Drake snorted. Has he abandoned that family, or do they exist? He scribbled in his bench book, and his hand cramped again.

Judge Drake nodded curtly to Mr. O'Brien, and Mr. O'Brien rose. "Would you tell the jury where and when you met Alexander McCaulay?" O'Brien asked Hughes.

"I met McCaulay at Buffalo Prairie, south of Henry House, early last winter. I met him three or four times, at intervals."

"And what transpired during those meetings?"

"I made an arrangement to go trapping in partnership with him. I was to furnish one part of the grub, and he was to furnish two parts."

"What opinion did you form of McCaulay at that time?"

"At first, he seemed to be trustworthy."

"I gather, then, that you later changed your mind. Is that so?"

"Yes! After we started travelling, his actions to his wife made me scared of him."

"What were those actions which first made you distrust McCaulay?"

"One day he lost his temper, and he whipped her." Hughes looked at the jury. His eyes were large and his voice was high.

Judge Drake snorted as he recorded Hughes' replies. Lying, he thought. He looked at the jury. All these years in court, he thought. I seem to see the same jury over and over. The worse the culprit, the more they believe. The law should dispense with juries. Judge Drake snorted again.

"Nevertheless," O'Brien said, "You and McCaulay went trapping. Did you catch beaver?"

"We got fourteen beaver."

"You say, 'We got fourteen beaver.' Tell the jury what you mean by that statement."

"McCaulay attended the traps, and I got the poles to stake them. I trusted to him. I was to get half."

"I gather that you believe he did not stick to that arrangement. Would you tell the jury what happened?"

"I had trouble with him at Swift Current Creek. I don't know what day it was. Day before the shooting, I think. It started over a saddle."

Judge Drake noticed that Hughes had warmed to his story. The judge looked sourly at the prisoner and then continued to write.

Hughes continued. "McCaulay wanted to use straps off my saddle. I couldn't let him do that. The saddle would a' been useless. He started to swear at me, so I turned to go. He ran at me with a knife. He could a' killed me, but Mrs. McCaulay caught him. She held him and talked to him in Cree while I got away. I went to my tent. When he got free, he came after me, and struck me with a knife. I dropped the saddle, and he took it. He said he would kill me. Then, he took my saddle and left. That night, I loaded the gun, but he didn't come."

As Judge Drake finished recording this statement, he cursed. "Why can't the woman speak English?" He mum-

159

bled. "The man can say whatever he pleases. No one can dispute it." The judge's right hand cramped.

"He didn't come that night," O'Brien prompted. "What did he do the next day?"

Jim Hughes continued: "In the morning I didn't know what he was doing. I wanted to make some coffee. I was opening a coffee can when I heard a shot. I jumped for my gun and ran out. McCaulay was coming for me. He was about twenty feet away, to the south and running at me. I hollered for him to halt. He had a knife. I thought he had a gun. I was pretty sure he had a gun. I aimed my gun, and I pulled the trigger."

"You pulled the trigger. What did you do then? O'Brien's voice was soft. He sounded awestruck.

"I stepped out from the bushes, and saw he was wounded. I was still scared, so I went to get his gun, but it wasn't there. I looked round, and saw it standing between the teepee poles. Mrs. McCaulay came running, and I told her to keep out of the way. I was scared McCaulay would attack me. She went back to her husband, and I saw that he was hurt pretty bad. I went to the teepee and got his gun and put both guns away in the tent. Then I went to him. He held out his hand. He wanted me to shake hands, so I did."

"What did he say to you?"

"He couldn't talk. He never said nothing."

"He never uttered a word? Where were the poor children all this time?" O'Brien's voice oozed sympathy.

Judge Drake scowled. "Poor children, indeed," he mumbled. He braced himself on the arm rests to ease the pain in his back.

"The children was inside the teepee poles. They was crying. I helped to move Alex there. I fixed up the blankets, and I got some water. I helped to care for him and the tots. I stayed there till his friends come."

"Mrs. McCaulay says she and McCaulay were saddling the horse when you fired. Is that true?"

"No! It ain't. McCaulay was about 60 feet away. There was willows round. I couldn't see McCaulay when he fell. There was a ridge in the way, about a foot up. There was no horse on the flat at all. The horses was tied behind the teepee."

"Would you tell the jury why you shot at McCaulay?"

"I was scared of him. If I didn't kill him, he would a' killed me."

"What did he do that made you think he would kill you?"

"I judged by his looks and how he acted. He tried to kill me the day before. I didn't think I was a match for him," Hughes whined. "He had a bad disposition. I don't think I could a' escaped him that day."

"And what did you do after you realized that he was so badly wounded?"

"I helped him as much as I could all the time after the shooting. I slept right there, in the teepee, every night except one. I didn't stay after he beat his wife."

"Mrs. McCaulay says that she had no food while you had plenty. Is that so?"

"I don't know why she says that. She wasn't in want at all."

Mr. O'Brien turned to the judge. "Those are all the questions I have, Your Honour," he said and returned to his seat.

Judge Drake snorted.

Maclean rose and began, "You are charged, in this court today, with murder. You admit that you shot at Alexander McCaulay, and yet you plead not guilty. Would you explain to the jury why you believe you are not guilty?"

"He was running at me, and he had something in his right hand. I couldn't see whether it was a knife or a gun."

"How close was he when you shot?"

"He was twenty-five, maybe thirty feet away."

"What did you do after you shot?"

"I went to the teepee right away, and I found his gun there. It wasn't in a case the way Mrs. McCaulay said."

"But neither was it in his hand. In fact, he had no weapon when you shot him. Is that not so?"

"He had something in his hand. I thought it was a gun."

"But he had no gun. What makes you so sure he had anything in his hand?"

"When I went to him, he handed me a knife."

"Surely you would be able to tell by his eyes if he was pointing a gun at you."

"I couldn't see his eyes."

"You say you heard a shot, and yet McCaulay had no gun. Who fired that shot?"

"I don't know who fired. I thought it was McCaulay."

"What did you do then?"

"I jumped for my gun and went out. He was running at me, and I was scared. I aimed at him, and I fired."

"And when you realized McCaulay had no gun, what did you think then?"

"He could a' fired it at his teepee, put down his gun and ran at me. He knew my gun was no account. I'm just a farmer. I started for the gold diggings. McCaulay must a' fired at the tent, put his gun down, and ran at me."

"Is this the first time you told this story? Didn't you tell it before the magistrate on the two occasions you appeared before him?"

"No! I didn't."

"Will you explain to the jury who fired the shot which frightened you so much that you shot a man?"

"First I thought McCaulay fired it. Then I thought Mrs. McCaulay did. There were cartridges at the teepee. The children might a' fired the gun if it was loaded, or threw a cartridge in the fire."

"Why did you fire so quickly. Surely you could have waited to assess the situation. McCaulay wasn't pointing a gun at you. You were the only one with a gun."

"My rifle is a magazine, but it doesn't work good. Sometimes, it misfires." Hughes looked around nervously.

Maclean turned to the judge. "No more questions," he said.

Judge Drake dismissed the prisoner. He noted that the pain in his back had eased and his hand had stopped cramping. "Are there any witnesses for the defence?" he asked.

Mr. O'Brien rose. "I have two, Your Honour," he said.

Alan Hampton took the stand and was sworn in. Mr. O'Brien began to question him.

"Do you know this man?" he asked indicating the prisoner.

"No sir! Alex McCaulay is the man I knew."

"Yes!" Mr. O'Brien said. "And what did you know about Mr. McCaulay?"

"His reputation was no good. He robbed people."

Mr. O'Brien had no more questions of the witness, and Maclean began, "You say you knew Mr. McCaulay. You mention his reputation. Did you know him well?"

"No, not well. I only knew him by sight."

"You only knew him by sight, and yet you said he robbed people. How do you know he robbed people?"

"The guys said he did. They said he robbed people and probably killed them, too."

Judge Drake snorted. "I might remind you," he said, "That you are in a court of law, and you are under oath. I wouldn't advise you to accuse anyone of theft unless you have proof."

"You say his reputation was not good," Maclean continued. "By what I hear in this town, not all reputations are good. In a small town, people talk. Last night, I heard of a man who went into a store and took some cartridges. When the owner asked him for the cartridges, he said that he wasn't a damn thief. But when threatened with the law, he produced the cartridges. I heard about a man who spends his time in a bawdy house with his favourite girl there. I think you know which man has this reputation. What would you say about a man who had a reputation like that? Now, about the robbing and killing, would you swear that Mr. McCaulay was the man the others were talking about?"

As Maclean continued, Alan Hampton looked around desperately. When Maclean glared at him for an answer, he mumbled without looking at him, "No, I don't know for sure." Then Hampton brightened and looked at Maclean. "I only knew McCaulay by his wife," he said.

"I bet he knew McCaulay's wife," the mime in the audience whispered, and a snicker rose from the jury and from the audience.

"Order in court!" Judge Drake barked as he rapped his gavel.

Next Fred Halford took the stand and was sworn in.

In answer to questions by the prosecutor, he established that he did not know Hughes, only McCaulay.

"I gather that you knew Alexander McCaulay very well. Is that so?"

"No. I only knew him by sight, but his reputation was very bad."

"Oh! I see, and who told you about his bad reputation?"

"I got it from Frank Jackson and another man."

"Well," said Maclean, "You might be surprised to learn, this is a court of law. A court of law does not deal in rumours. What are you doing in the witness stand swearing to the character of a man you know nothing about?"

"When Martin asked me to come, I told him I knew nothing of the man. I told him I never met McCaulay. I only know what I picked up by the campfire."

"Well, what you pick up around the campfire isn't evidence in this or any other court. You might remember that in future," Judge Drake interposed. "Unless Maclean has further questions, you are free to leave the court."

Jurymen looked up to the ceiling. A voice in the audience mumbled, "Stupid bugger!" and a general murmur erupted through the court.

Judge Drake pounded his gavel. "ORDER IN COURT!" he bellowed. "Remove that man!" he ordered, indicating one man in the crowd. Sheriff Redgrave stepped forward, and the man left the court.

Quiet ensued, and at O'Brien's request, Judge Drake recalled Dr. Taylor who was questioned by O'Brien. The doctor stated: "No, the tongue was not injured, but the attachment to the lower jaw was torn asunder. The lower jaw was broken."

"In your opinion, could a man so injured speak?"

"No!" said the doctor. "I do not think a man so suffering could speak. He could, I believe, articulate only guttural sounds."

Dr. Taylor was excused, and Mr. O'Brien requested Mr. Price be recalled. "You will remember the area around the camp where McCaulay's teepee and Mr. Hughes tent were located. Would you say that area was completely clear of growth?" Mr. O'Brien asked him.

"Not completely clear. There were a few scattered little willows," Kid replied.

"Thank you," said Thomas O'Brien. "That will be all."

"Witness excused," said the judge. "Any further witnesses?"

"No, Your Honour. No further witnesses."

The sun had set behind the mountains, and carbide chandeliers lit the hall. Judge Drake was tired. The trial had been in session for nearly five hours. He adjourned the court till ten o'clock the next morning. All the evidence was in and examined. The plea from the defence and the prosecutor remained, as well as the judge's summation. He was too tired even to think of it now, but he would awake in the night and give it due consideration. Judge Drake rose and rushed to the urinal.

The jury went into seclusion; Maclean and Mr. O'Brien went to their separate dinners. The crowd dispersed into the damp night. Some travelled to homes warmed by wood heaters and lit by candles or kerosene lamps. These men told of the day's proceedings to eager wives and families. Others stayed in restaurants, saloons and hotel lobbies, next to barrel heaters glowing with warmth.

As the crowd started to move, Adelaide quickly slipped out of the hall and hurried back to her children. Kid, freed from the witness box looked around for her, for Dan, and finally found Jack. "What went on in that court room?" Kid asked.

Jack nodded toward the saloon, they turned, and as they walked through the door, they saw a group of men push two tables together and pull up chairs around. Kid picked a small table in the corner, his back to the wall.

Someone shouted, "Well! Here's the good doctor!"

As Kid bristled and tensed to jump, Jack pushed him back. "Cool it!" Jack commanded. "We're here to find out what happened. Remember?" Kid sank back in his chair. Jack settled down between him and the crowd, and ordered two beers.

The men in the group each bought a round, so there was hardly room on the tables to hold all the beer. Conversation became more raucous by the minute.

Kid slumped in his chair with fists clenched and listened. The conversation was about cutting an Indian in the belly after using the knife to trim a horse's hooves, an Indian who could still talk with half his jaw missing, an Indian who politely shook hands and thanked the man who shot him.

"Time we left," Jack said as he rose and steered Kid away from the gossip.

As they wended their way to the door, they heard, "The man who spends his time at a bawdy house! Maclean was so busy needling Hampton, he didn't noticed how many faces turned red." A noisy burst of laughter and then, "Rumour around a campfire! That is not evidence in this or any other court!"

"Shit!" Kid said. "Is that what Maclean said? Is that what the judge said? Maclean lost the case! Sounds like a Sunday school teacher! Half those jurymen go to the same whorehouse as Hampton does. Where did those fools come from? If Maclean hadn't already lost the case, the judge would have. How else does a prospector find out about danger other than to listen to the men who've been there. Why didn't Drake point out that Hampton hadn't been there. Those jurymen must have thought the judge was daft."

"Those men aren't the jury, Kid," Jack said. "It's not over yet. We'll go have some dinner, and then you go back to your room and get some rest. Tomorrow is another day."

Kid mumbled as he tramped furiously down the street toward the restaurant. "Then it was my turn! I was right up there with the big boys! I felt pretty sure of myself when I walked up to that stand. I had Doc to back me up, and I felt sprightly as you please. I'd taken my dress pants, waistcoat, and jacket out of the tin trunk where I keep them from the mice, moths, and squirrels, and I'd hung them in the wind for three days to get rid of the smell of moth balls. Then I took them to the Chinese laundry to be cleaned and pressed. My white shirt was threadbare, so I bought a new one and a snazzy tie. I'd gone to the barber for a shave, and a trim to my mustache and my hair. I was dressed like a ham for Sunday dinner.

"I gave Griffith a friendly nod, ignored O'Brien, and smiled to my audience. I was in top form, pleased with myself for what I'd done. I thought I'd done a damn fine thing, and I wanted people to know about it. I didn't know what was coming, and I continued to tell every damning detail. After I had told everything there was to tell, I got the O'Brien treatment."

Kid and Jack went, had their dinner and returned to their rooms, and one by one the men in the saloon left the warm fireside and the hot words and went to chilly rooms and beds piled with blankets.

Chapter XXVIII

At ten sharp, Thomas O'Brien rose to plead in defence of James Hughes. "Good morning Your Honour," he said nodding to Judge Drake. "I trust you have had a comfortable night."

He nodded again, this time towards the jury, smiled slightly, then assumed a serious expression and began to speak. "I hope you have arrived in this courtroom refreshed and ready to decide the fate of the man here before you, Mr. Hughes, who is a guest in our fair country from the United States. Since Mr. Hughes left his home in Arkansas City, nearly two years have passed," Thomas O'Brien began softly. "The poor prisoner is a much older and sadder man. He left behind a wife he adores and five lovely children. Often, when I go to his bare cell hoping to discuss this unfortunate case, he talks of nothing but the family he left in Arkansas. Especially, he talks of his youngest daughter, a girl of three whom, he is afraid, no longer remembers him. And then he thinks of the family in the north who were robbed of their father by misadventure, and he wonders sadly why he could not have treated those lovely children better than he did."

Thomas O'Brien continued in this manner. He told of James Hughes travelling north and of his winter in a lonely cabin.

"Finally as spring neared, Hughes met the McCaulay family," he continued. "The two small children attracted him, away as he was from his own wee tots for nearly a full year, and (what could be worse?) away from civilization for much of that time. Blinded by his need for family he found them all charming, even the father. The children, as children will, adored the scoundrel, their papa, and this caused the prisoner to see McCaulay through their innocent eyes.

"Jim made a contract to go trapping with the McCaulay family. McCaulay would supply the food for his wife and children, and Jim and McCaulay would trap together and divide the pelts. Half would go to each." Thomas O'Brien spoke softly and earnestly.

"The party was not long on the way when McCaulay's true nature began to manifest itself. McCaulay was cranky and cruel to his horses. He used the horse whip on the horses, and he turned from the horses, and he used the same whip on his poor wife. The poor babies cowered in fear.

"Nonetheless, Jim went trapping with McCaulay. Jim was fearful the whole time of crossing McCaulay lest the man explode in a violent temper. When beaver season finished, their catch amounted to fourteen pelts, half of which, according to their agreement, belonged to Jim. However, when McCaulay decided he would separate from Mr. Hughes and return to Henry House, the trouble began. McCaulay demanded the straps off Jim's saddle to fix his own. Jim could not allow McCaulay to leave him, so far from civilization, with a useless saddle. McCaulay began to swear. Without warning, he attacked Jim with a knife. The poor man's life was spared by the intervention of McCaulay's gentle wife who flung her arms around her husband, pleaded with him, and held him until Jim escaped to his own tent. Alone in his tent, the frightened man loaded his gun and watched and waited throughout the night. After those hours of darkness, of expecting attack at any moment, while preparing for a day of he knew not what, the prisoner was opening a can of coffee. Suddenly, the crack of a rifle broke the stillness. Mr. Hughes grabbed his gun, inserted a cartridge, and rushed from the tent to see McCaulay coming at him. He thought McCaulay had a gun.

"Consider Jim's position. He held a gun with one cartridge. He thought he had one chance, but he could not be sure. He could not trust his gun. Sometimes, that gun misfired. A crazed man was approaching. He raised his gun. 'Halt!' he yelled. McCaulay continued to run toward him. What could Jim do? He fired.

"When he saw what a terrible thing he had done, Jim helped Mrs. McCaulay carry her wounded husband to the teepee and did everything he could to help the poor misguided man. Jim sat by McCaulay's bed day and night until help arrived.

"You have heard much testimony on behalf of the Crown. I beseech you—consider the probabilities before you accept any testimony. I beg that your verdict be given, not in accordance with the sworn testimony, but only by that which you can believe.

"From the evidence adduced, no motive whatsoever was shown for one of the most heinous crimes which can be charged to any man. Now, I would like you to consider the position of these two men in that valley, distant from all civilized intrusion.

"Jim Hughes, here before you today, owned a complete outfit, good strong saddle and pack horses, all the gear he could use; tent, clothing, bedding, and food enough for the summer even though miles from any source. He was on his way to the Yukon; he had a plan and the means to implement it.

"Now, consider the position of the deceased. Again, miles from any intervention, he had travelled into the country with nothing, not even food enough for his family. His wife was reduced to smoking beaver meat over willow twigs for their larder. He had a few skinny horses and a moldy teepee. He had nothing! Nothing! Of the two men, I suggest, the deceased was the only one who would benefit from committing a crime.

"The only person who claimed to be an eye witness, Mrs. McCaulay, must surely be mistaken, as the course the bullet was proven to have taken, from the doctor's sworn testimony, bore out the prisoner's story absolutely. If Mrs. McCaulay was mistaken in this, it is the duty of the jury to reject her testimony altogether.

"You will remember the testimony admitted by the Crown, that McCaulay beckoned the prisoner to approach him immediately after the shooting took place and shook him by the hand. Gentlemen of the jury, that would not be the conduct of a missionary. Nor would it be the act of a cold blooded murderer after shooting his victim.

"That testimony in itself would justify you, as jurymen, to discard any testimony from such a witness."

The jury nodded in agreement.

Kid jumped to his feet. "That bloody Hughes said they shook hands too," he shouted. "What about that?"

"ORDER IN THE COURT," Judge Drake banged repeatedly. "I will not allow such conduct in the Queen's Court. Remove that man!" he commanded. Constable Redgrave rushed forward, gun in hand. Kid struck out, slapped the gun from his hand, and knocked the aged constable to the floor. Two husky men rushed to Redgrave's aid. Dan dove and grabbed one man by the feet. A dozen men joined the foray. Adelaide crept away. She hid behind a pillar. A mad struggle ensued. Blows flew. The gun was kicked across the hall. Someone shouted, "STOP OR I'LL SHOOT!"

Everything stopped.

In that moment, both Kid and Dan were pinned to the floor, and with the aid of husky men, Constable Redgrave, with his gun restored, escorted Kid and Dan from the room.

O'Brien looked smug. The court came to order and he continued: "Now, if you would consider the testimony of the two men, Price and Noyes, you might decide to reject it altogether. Consider these men, who swore on the Bible, as they did, that the deceased, injured as he was with part of his jaw missing, talked to them. As witnesses Price and Noyes are not credible. No man could ever utter a word whose tongue and jaw were as badly injured as was shown by Doctor Taylor's evidence."

Mr. O'Brien gathered up his papers, nodded to the judge, smiled at the jury, and sat down.

Chapter XXIX

Before ten that morning, Adelaide sat with Kid and Dan at the back of the courtroom. In the crowded room, the seats next them were empty. Throughout O'Brien's delivery, she understood a few words: *McCaulay, Noyes, Price, horse, beaver, pelt, trap, gun.* These words she understood in English. She watched faces. She could see that the people adored O'Brien. She knew that was not good. Hughes looked very somber, but he was not frightened. He should be frightened, she thought.

While O'Brien spoke, she could read boredom in the judge's every action: he rifled through papers, stared out the window, tapped his fingers. She looked around at the crowd again. Whenever anyone looked at her, she felt uneasy. She saw no sympathy in their faces. She looked at Kid. He watched O'Brien. She could see the fury in Kid's eyes. His fists were clenched. She looked at Dan. He looked at Kid, at O'Brien, at the jury. She knew he was as confused as she.

Adelaide saw the jurymen nod. She heard Kid burst out. She looked at him and listened; she understood bloody, Hughes, and hands. She heard the judge and looked to him, so she didn't see the constable come. When the fight started, she rushed for cover and then froze. She wanted to help, but the time wasn't right. Nothing she could do would defeat the mob. She watched as they took Kid and Dan away.

Now, she was alone. She stayed behind the pillar. She must learn all she could. She saw the grins on faces in the crowd as Dan and Kid disappeared, saw the smug face of O'Brien and saw the look of distaste the judge bestowed on O'Brien.

As Thomas O'Brien spoke, she understood a few words. When Mr. O'Brien completed his oration, she heard a pleased "Ahhhh!" burst from a dozen throats.

Adelaide watched as Maclean rose and addressed the judge and the jury. She must listen for the words she understood. She must read people's faces and their actions.

Chapter XXX

Maclean had witnessed the hypnotic spell created by O'Brien. Uncomplicated facts, he decided, were needed to break that spell.

"Your Honour," Maclean said, "honourable men of the jury, Mr. O'Brien has given an eloquent and able appeal on behalf of the prisoner. No counsel could have done more. Unfortunately, he was defending a guilty man.

"The prisoner admitted under oath that he shot the man. Two witnesses, both Mr. Price and Mr. Noyes, testified that the prisoner admitted the same to them. Therefore, he is guilty, if not of murder, then of manslaughter. Under Canadian law if anyone shoots another, and if it can be proven the shot was fired in self defence, the charge can be reduced to manslaughter even though the shot was intentional. If there is not evidence of self defence and the shot was not accidental, then the charge is murder. In the case before you, the prosecution has proven the shot was not fired in self defence, but fired with deliberate intent.

"The prisoner admits that the deceased did not have a gun. The gun was in the teepee at least thirty feet away. Since he had a gun in hand and the prisoner did not, presenting the gun was threat enough to keep the man at bay. If he felt threatened, he could have confiscated the man's ammunition.

"Dr. Taylor, in his testimony, has proven that the deceased was not running when the shot was fired, that he was in fact in a stooped position. He was not even full face towards the prisoner; the bullet pierced the man's hat and destroyed the right side of his face. It re-entered his chest and travelled through the length of his chest to lodge in his stomach. Ask yourselves if he could have been running. Ask yourself if, running, he would have continued to run into a loaded rifle.

"The defence presented you with two witnesses who attempted to destroy the character of the victim. These witnesses admit they did not know the deceased but were relying on rumour. The defence did not trace these rumours to their source and bring that source in so it could be examined. The defence only presented you with an unsubstantiated rumour.

"The prosecution, on the other hand, presented you with two witnesses who knew the deceased. The first witness, Mr. Price, knew Alexander McCaulay, lived with him for the better part of a year, and worked with him. Mr. Price stated: 'I found McCaulay to be a man of good disposition; we remained the best of friends.' The second witness, Mr. Noyes, stated he knew McCaulay for ten years; he lived in the same community with Mr. McCaulay and did business with him. Noyes stated McCaulay's reputation was good in every way. A man's true reputation is better gauged by those who know him well than by strangers.

"Mr. Noyes stated that the condition he found the victim and his family in was not good. Although the prisoner denied it, Mr. Noyes, Mr. Price, Mr. Evans, and Mrs. McCaulay all stated that the family had only beaver meat and a little flour; whereas, they stated, the prisoner was well supplied with food.

"Mrs. McCaulay stated: 'there was no quarrel the day of the shooting; the quarrel the day before was about a saddle; McCaulay returned that saddle to the prisoner the evening before the shooting.' Her account of the shooting is substantiated by Dr. Taylor's evidence regarding the path of the bullet."

Maclean continued in this fashion examining each piece of evidence for the jury to consider. Finally, after carefully making his case, he retired.

Chapter XXXI

Both the defence and the prosecution had stated their case. It was now time for Judge Drake to make his summation. Although O'Brien's address had bored him into lethargy, the disturbance had roused the judge. Once quiet was restored in the court and O'Brien began to speak again, he watched the man's cocky manner, and remembered his own antipathy towards Mr. O'Brien. The spunk of those men challenging him in court, he thought. The convictions he had established from watching the witnesses and listening to their evidence strengthened. As he spoke, he thought about the murderer, his defendant, and the stupidity of the jury. He glared contemptuously at the jurymen and stared them down.

"History," he said, "will record this event as a sad tragedy. The parties arrived at Swift Current and went trapping. The deceased prepared to return home and had collected his horses. He had saddled all but the last one when the fatal shot was fired. According to his wife's evidence, he was fastening the cinch of his saddle to a horse which his wife was holding when the shot was fired. There had been no quarrel that day of any sort. None of the prisoner's provisions had been packed up. The deceased's rifle was in a case thirty or forty feet away in the teepee, and the children were there. The teepee had been stripped. Only the poles remained."

As Judge Drake spoke his fury subsided, but his manner and his voice were stern. No chuckles interrupted him. No faces erupted in mirth. Hughes appeared to be frightened. The judge continued to state the case for the prosecution much as presented by Maclean. He pointed out that the prisoner had admitted to the shooting; he stated that the doctor's testimony regarding the course of the bullet precluded the possibility that the deceased was running toward Hughes; he outlined the inconsistencies in Hughes' testimony, and he continued on at some length.

Finally he concluded with the words:

"The prisoner was twice before a magistrate and never a word about self-defence. It is hardly credible that, if he was in fear of his life, he would not have previously told it to these men. The law with regard to self-defence being an excuse for homicide is this: if a person is attacked by another with a deadly weapon and is in such a position that his life is in danger, he may protect himself, and then reduce what would be murder to manslaughter, but must satisfy you of the imminence of the danger. Here, no weapon was seen in the deceased's hand. His rifle was away. The statement of the defendant hearing a shot is improbable.

"I may point out to you that on this indication, you can bring in one of three verdicts, guilty, not guilty, or guilty of manslaughter."

With his final sentence, Judge Drake dismissed the court. The day was at noon. The jurymen—a clutch of prospectors, one seasonally unemployed mining recorder-cum-clerk-cum-special-constable-cum-gaoler, one barber, and all—went into retirement, and the crowd filed out to await their verdict.

Chapter XXXII

Adelaide had watched as Maclean stood and began to speak. Maclean looked at Thomas O'Brien, and said something which caused the jury and the audience to nod in agreement, but after that, eyes glazed over. People in the audience fidgeted. Every member of the jury slumped in his seat and waited. People were not listening to Maclean. She saw Judge Drake's eyes flash as he watched the jury. He clamped his jaw, then let out a disgusted snort.

Members of the jury straightened in their seats and assumed an attitude of attention. Members of the crowd twisted their mouths in wry smiles; quiet chuckles emitted from the throng. Sighs filled the air as Maclean continued to speak, and more sighs as he resumed his seat.

Adelaide felt the atmosphere change as Judge Drake began to speak. She saw that he was contemptuous of the jury. She watched him stare until the jurymen lowered their eyes. She heard the fury in his voice. The men are afraid of him, but they don't like him any better than he likes them, she concluded.

When Judge Drake finished speaking and the crowd wandered out into the lobby and then the bar, Adelaide followed. As the door to the bar opened, Adelaide looked through and saw men bringing drinks, saw men stare back at her. This, she knew, was a place where women did not go, were not allowed to go. During the summer when she came to town, men went into this place. Women did not. Adelaide left and went to check her horse where it was tied with horses belonging to Kid and Dan. The horses were still there, but Kid and Dan nowhere in sight. Adelaide searched up and down the street and over by the river. The crowd, even those who did not go for drinks, hung around, so perhaps there would be more. She saw some people go for tea and food. She took bannock and dried meat from her saddle bag and ate.

The sun had hardly moved in the sky when the clerk opened the courtroom door and the crowd filed in. Adelaide followed.

When quiet filled the room, the judge spoke to the man from the jury, and the juryman answered.

As the man's voice faded, Adelaide could see terrible anger in Judge Drake's face. He said a few words, rose, turned, strode to the side door, and disappeared. Adelaide watched as the judge and then Maclean left. She watched the crowd in the courtroom stir. Someone sighed. A man stepped forward, clapped O'Brien on the back, and emitted a loud "Hah! Good work!" Cheers rose from every throat.

Cheers echoed and re-echoed through the court. Cheers wafted Thomas O'Brien into the November afternoon. Down the Golden street, he strutted, a prosperous and successful man surrounded by friends.

Adelaide stood apart. Stoically, she held her head high, and clutched her blanket about her. She watched the crowd cluster around O'Brien, watched Hughes push up close to O'Brien and began to talk, heard men interrupt Hughes, and saw them shove him aside. She listened to the cheers, watched the crowd with O'Brien and Hughes move down the aisle and out into the street. As she watched, she seethed inwardly.

I did not see Hughes dragged away.

I did not stay in this nothing place till there was no more summer for this, this nothing.

I did not ride on a trail that did not take me home,

I did not bring my children through a summer of no happiness,

I did not make my pony walk on a trail that could not hold him up,

I did not build my campfire in a land I did not know, to *not* see Hughes dance upon the air.

When I came here, no Redcoats wanted to hear my story, but Kid said I must stay. "That bastard has to hang," he said. He brought Dan to tell me what he said. "We would have to bring you back. You have to tell them," Dan said. Dan said I must stay. Only I could tell them.

I did not need to come to this valley. I could go home. They did not need to bring Hughes here. Hughes wanted to go to the north. Grandfather, Musom, knows the ways of the rivers, the mountains, and the valleys. Musom would guide Hughes to the north. Above a cliff on some narrow trail, or in some deep river, a bee would sting Hughes' horse. A bee would do that for Musom.

I stayed. I picked berries, I dried fish, tanned caribou hide, sewed. All the summer days passed by. I told them. In court, I told whiteman, and still Kid said I must stay. The people broke camp and rode away, rode home and left me.

Kid said he would go with me. Dan would go with me. I stayed again. Who is here to go with me now?

When the hall had emptied, and all the people were gone, Adelaide raised her head and strode silently into the November day. She mounted her horse and rode toward the north.

Early the next morning a hunter saw some Indians. Later at the bar, he told the boys he saw a squaw on a sway back mare with a skinny colt dragging behind. The squaw was dressed in a dirty black skirt and wrapped in an old red blanket. She had a papoose on with her, and a scrawny boy in buckskin followed on a wall-eyed cayuse. Another cayuse with filthy canvas packs, and a bunch of half-starved, mangy dogs, that's what he saw. The one thing he liked about the winter was that the Indians left the country.

Chapter XXXIII

The weather in the east Kootenay, as recorded by R. D. Davies, observer at the weather station at Donald, was cloudy but comparatively mild for the month of November. Some rain fell, but although there had been slush in mid-October, the first real snow fell on November 30th. The temperature hovered around freezing at nights but rose several degrees during the day. For the first four nights after the trial, the weather had improved, and the following days were fairly warm but cloudy.

The trail, after it passed the Wait-a-bit, traversed some high country, but the weather would not have stopped someone determined to go. Possibly, Adelaide started then on the long journey.

There is a story of those early days, told by a trapper. Was it the year 1899? Earlier? Or later? He couldn't remember. It was the fall of the year, early November. He remembered that. He purchased his supplies for the winter, loaded his canoe. He had to make the usual portages before he poled up the Canoe River. Trapping for the winter was his intent.

Almost at Goat Lick Creek, in a cold rain, thinking to stop for the day, he was, when he saw smoke from a campfire. He poled on up and beached his canoe.

There, in that camp, was a young native woman. Beautiful, she was, and proud. She was maybe twenty—not much more. Two small children huddled under a tree. A fire sputtered. She had a canvas fly to keep the weather off and a spruce bough bed. Rain drizzled down. The trees, the bushes, the canvas, everything dripped. All by herself, she was—no man—no one else. She was travelling with horses. Wouldn't have travelled with horses himself. Not many people would. Not that late in the year.

Come to think of it, it must have been 1899—the year after that fellow salted Swift Current Creek. The year of the big gold rush, it was. Men, horses, pack horses, men on foot, passed by in droves—all summer long. The trail was in an awful mess— mud to the horse's knees.

The woman was waiting—waiting for frost to stiffen up the trail. Cooking dinner,—a squirrel carcass boiling in a pail— some roots, something added, and berries, dried berries, a handful of flour to thicken the gravy.

He stopped, made his own camp. Next day, he went on to the Goat Lick, and he shot some goat. Three of them, he shot.

Skinned them out in a flash, she did. Fried the liver. Liver and bannock, they ate.

She made drying racks out of poles. He helped her get the poles and wood for the fire. She cut that goat into strips, put it to dry, and pounded it. Making pemmican, she was. Some for her. Some for him. Cracked the bones. Boiled them for the marrow. The broth, they drank, him, her, and the kids, her kids. Them kids sat back and rubbed their full bellies and smiled. Everybody was happy.

Sang while she worked, "Hiya, hiya, hiya, hi. . !"

The kids come running. Swing them up in the air, she would. Sit them down and tell them stories. Wide-eyed, they sat. Sometimes repeated what she said and laughed. All of them laughed, but sometimes he saw her cry, cry and pound the pemmican harder.

Used every bit of that goat—head, heart, liver; all but the hooves. Even saved the horns for something.

He shot a couple more goat. Not much meat on a goat. She made bags from some of the skins, bags to put the pemmican in. Sewed it up tight as a drum.

Hated to leave her there. Thought about her all winter, he did.

She was heading back to Wood River, or thereabouts. She didn't speak English so he was never quite sure. But she never did travel much farther up the trail. He watched for her when he got to his trap line—watched for the tracks, but there never were any.

Chapter XXXIV

Sheriff Redgrave opened the door to the lock-up and threw his prisoners in. He hadn't even had time to air the place after he freed Hughes. His second wife wasn't as accommodating as the first, and she wouldn't be happy to cook for two prisoners. He would be giving them lumpy porridge and dry crusts. When the time came, he added *The Golden Era* to that menu. He considered it their just dessert after that fracas in court.

Giant headlines—Not Guilty—followed by a three column spread. That should give them something to think about. The sheriff knew what they would read in that paper:

> Dr. Taylor described the wounds which would be of a fatal nature. The doctor found indications of pleurisy, but with proper care, McCaulay might have lived. The doctor said a cut in the abdomen by an unprofessional man might cause death as there would be a great danger of blood poisoning. Judge Drake disallowed O'Brien's objection to Price as witness, and refused O'Brien's request to reserve a case on this point. However, when Price resumed his evidence, he was severely cross-examined.

This and more they read. They would have to read through nearly a column about the grand jury and their petitions before they found what they were looking for. Then Dr. Taylor's evidence pointed the finger. Let them think about that.

Then they would read a word for word account of Adelaide's testimony, ending with a description of Adelaide crying at the sight of Alex's blood-stained shirt. They would learn the unhappy effect of the law on Indians who didn't mend their ways.

Hughes' testimony appeared in full—more food for thought.

Even Maclean, Deputy Attorney-General of the province, had complimented Thomas O'Brien, Counsel for the Defence, on his eloquent and able appeal on behalf of the prisoner. He felt satisfied no counsel could have done more.

Mr. O'Brien's able appeal had been documented for good citizen's to savour. His Lordship charged the jury in a strong and forcible manner desiring them to return a verdict of guilty. After about an hour's thought, the jury returned a verdict of not guilty, and the crowd erupted in cheers for O'Brien.

When the sheriff returned for the dirty dishes, Price and Noyes were reading the paper, and they were certainly subdued. Price requested that Sheriff Redgrave send word asking Griffith to find Adelaide. Price said she had no food, and would not know what to do as she was alone. Griffith sent back word that Adelaide's cabin was empty, and he did not know where to find her.

Clara, Alan, and Percy sat on their favourite bench overlooking the bay. In the warm sunshine, they felt refreshed by a cool breeze off the water. Clara and Alan knew the time neared for their to return to Salt Lake City, and they hadn't heard all of Percy's story. They begged him to continue.

"When Redgrave came to unlock that door," Percy began, "We were as meek as kittens, and stayed that way until we were out of town. Then, we went to Adelaide's cabin, and it was, indeed, empty. No sign, no message of any kind. Gone.

"We made quiet inquiries around town, and then we headed north as quickly as we could. It still was possible to travel with horses though heavy snow could come at any time.

"We checked north of town and at Donald. When we got beyond the settlements, we saw signs that somebody had travelled that way—horse droppings, extinguished fires, nibbled branches. The signs continued down the Columbia and up the Canoe River. After some place near Ptarmigan Creek, we found no more signs. We doubled back to where we had noticed that someone had camped for a few days, but we found nothing, nothing the children had dropped, no other trail, nothing. Still, we were sure Adelaide had camped there. We were certain she hadn't gone back. We had to go on and hope. If we tarried and the snow came, the horses wouldn't survive.

"By the time we got to the Starvation Camp, we were travelling in snow, so we put the horses to pasture and went on to Swift Current Creek on snowshoes. No Adelaide. No sign. No message. Dan snowshoed on to Henry House and then home to Edmonton, and I returned to the cabin at Starvation Flats.

"Jack arrived the next day, but he had heard nothing of Adelaide. That winter I snowshoed to Henry House."

"Henry House!" Clara interrupted. "How long did that take? Wasn't Henry House on the other side of the Rockies?"

"It took me a good week, maybe ten days. I was lucky in the weather. But, at Henry House when I spoke, nobody there understood me, although I was sure some spoke English.

"I'd been back at our cabin for a couple of weeks, but the thought that she might be lost in the mountains haunted me, so I snowshoed to Golden. In Golden, people shrugged. The Indian woman was gone. Someone told me about an Indian trail through the mountains.

"Travelling back to Starvation Flats, I met a trapper who had seen her near Ptarmigan Creek. I thought of the Indian trail. It couldn't follow up the Ptarmigan Creek. That was impossible to imagine. Ptarmigan Creek started into a canyon so steep you had to take off your snowshoes to climb. But Adelaide went somewhere. Her trail disappeared near the Ptarmigan. The Ptarmigan headwaters rose near the headwaters of the Fraser River. The pass was in some pretty high country—and probably snow that time of year, maybe not too much. There was a trail from somewhere near Yellowhead Lake up the Fraser that passed the headwaters of the Ptarmigan. But, I still can't picture travelling up that canyon.

"I looked for Adelaide for years. Spoke to every Cree I met, but the ones from Henry House weren't friendly with me any more.

"In 1910, the North West Mounted Police rounded up the Indians at Henry House because the flats had been included in Jasper Park. Some of the folks were paid for their land, not many—Moberlys—a few others. They were considered squatters—no titles.

"I don't know whether Adelaide was among them. By the time I heard, folks were gone. She would have taken another partner by then and taken that man's name. Mosie and Mary would go by that name too." He hesitated and then breathed a deep and tired sigh. "At least that is what I hope. I hope she made it through the mountains, but I'll never know. Sometimes it just eats me up—the way she was treated."

"Oh Percy!" Clara sniffed and wiped her eyes. "To think, had you found her, had you married, you would have had a family around you now."

"I would have had a family that was subject to prejudice from my neighbors and probably from the Indians because their dad was white. I would have been called a squaw man, and spent my life punching guys out for that. I assure you, Clara, Adelaide and her children would be better off among their own people." As Percy finished, he looked sadder than Clara had ever seen him.

"I don't know what the answer is. Sometimes folks are so cruel." Clara wept for Percy and for the family she had never known.

"It takes time," Alan said, "a long time for people to change."

"Come home with us," Clara beseeched. "You can't live out your life here, without family, alone."

"I do want more than anything to meet the huge family— the Price clan. I want to meet every one." Percy answered.

He sat quietly. The thoughts of returning slowly cheered him. He thought about each brother and each sister and the families they had raised. He thought of how much he had enjoyed meeting Alan. Alan had a wonderful life. When Percy left home, he had wanted to become a doctor. He searched for gold to pay for his education.

Some of his nephews and nieces, like Alan, had acquired an education, were teachers, preachers, nurses and photographers. Some had stayed on homesteads and were farmers. He thought about his sister's boy, Charles Percy, named for him. Charles Percy was a preacher. Of course, he was retired now, but Percy thought he would have to clean up his language before he met Charles Percy. He thought about Bob, his oldest nephew whose grandson farmed the old homestead. He hoped the grandson would welcome him. Some of his kin were drifters. He wanted to meet them all.

Clara chattered happily as they walked back to the residence. When they arrived, she checked through Percy's things. A small U-Haul would move everything.

The next morning when Percy saw Clara, he suggested that Alan might be able to rent a cabin in the mountains for him. Percy had been a bachelor all his life, and he wouldn't feel comfortable in someone else's home.

Two days later as Clara and Alan were packing their car to leave, Percy said, "Don't rent that cabin till I write that I am ready.

"As soon as I collect a grubstake and gear, and finish one more trip for gold, I will come to you," Percy promised.

Epilogue

For seventy years until it disappeared during highway construction, a small wooden cross marked a grave on a stony shore of a stream in the Rocky Mountains. Settlers could tell you that buried there was a young trapper, part native, shot by another man. Why that shot was fired, they could only guess. Some said it was an act of self defense; some said it was done in a fit of temper; others mentioned desperation—that the Native meant to leave an old man without provisions. Still others said the prospector fired with cold calculation—the Indian would not guide the man to the Yukon, so his woman must, or starve. People say he who fired the fatal shot was acquitted of any crime and, after the trial, returned from whence he came.

At Henry House Flats, east of the Rocky Mountains where the Maligne River flows into the Athabasca, two log cabins with dovetail corners still stand. The meadows, once fenced and planted to hay and oats, are now grazed by elk. This was once the home of Ewan Moberly and part of the community where the trapper and his family lived. The grave of Susan Cardinal, Ewan Moberly's mother, is fenced and marked with a cross. No other signs of that community have survived.

Housed in the British Columbia Provincial Archives is the testimony of Jim Hughes, the man who fired the shot; of Adelaide McCaulay, the widow and witness, and of the men who happened on the scene. On microfilm are the newspapers of the day.

Stories which have survived tell of Kid Price blamed in court for McCaulay's death; of a native woman with her children travelling up the Canoe River as winter approached. No record exists of any money allotted to provide for Adelaide McCaulay's stay in the Columbia River Valley while she awaited the trial, except for a meagre twenty-three dollars for provisions, nor any money allotted to help her return home.

In the spring of 1993, I began a research of early exploration and travel on the Canoe River, a river swallowed by a British Columbia Hydro reservoir in the 1960s and 70s. My attempts were augmented by generous access to the research of Shirley Klettl, Valemount Historic Society, and Tom Peterson, Jasper Historic Society.

I wrote to the British Columbia Archives in Victoria and received an encouraging reply from David Mattison, Curator, together with some photocopies and a list of further material available in the archives.

By September, I was hooked on research, and I went to Victoria to examine the records and see what I could find. With the aid of David Mattison, Archivist, and Brent McBride of Client Services I found their treasures and, among them, three letters concerning the first Supreme Court trial in Golden, the trial of James Hughes, charged with the murder, near Mount Robson, of Alexander McCaulay. Two of these letters were from the magistrate and reported the shooting and then the death of McCaulay. The magistrate had forwarded pertinent data regarding the arrest and preliminary hearing, requested permission to pay expenses, and warned of the huge costs that could accrue because of the distances involved. The third letter was from counsel for the defence to the attorney-general. Counsel for the defence seemed to offer to make a deal.

I inquired of Mr. McBride whether there might be further records. He showed me microfilm of early newspapers. Golden's paper, *The Golden Era* for 1898 and 1899, he told me, was a likely source. Since *The Golden Era* was a weekly, and all the news was on the first page, it was easy enough to find all the references to my topic as well as a forgotten gold rush to Tête Jaune which coincided with the murder.

The paper quoted politicians and their promises and reported mining and prospecting news. Item after item told about gold at Tête Jaune Cache. In an area beyond Swift Current Creek, one article stated, gold-bearing quartz extended for six or seven miles. The gold was visible to the naked eye. Swift Current Creek yielded up to thirty cents to the pan. No work had been done yet on bedrock, but the gold in the rim rock was very coarse.

Then in the paper of July 14, 1899, I read about the shooting at Tête Jaune Cache. Three subsequent papers told about the shooting and death of McCaulay and the hearings and trial of Jim Hughes.

By late fall of 1899 the gold and the murder at Tête Jaune Cache were no longer mentioned. The big news then was of the trouble in South Africa.

Mr. Mattison, of the British Columbia Archives, sent me photocopies of the contents of a huge file which included several typed copies of the depositions recorded by the magistrate at the two preliminary hearings. One set of copies, that of the Crown counsel, had points for the prosecution highlighted. On the back of another were notes from the Supreme Court trial handwritten by the Crown counsel. There was evidence from an undisclosed source as well as a note regarding the reliability of the witnesses for the defence. Enclosed, also, were copies of pages from the judge's bench book—his notes at the Supreme Court Trial.

When I showed the research to my husband, Angus, he knew much of the story. When Angus was a child, his dad told stories. His dad told of a guide who got shot, a guide who refused to take a prospector to the Yukon. He told of the man who tended the dying guide, removed the bullet, and then was blamed in court for the guide's death. He told of the judge who instructed the jury on how to find, and he told of the jury who wouldn't listen. He told of the lawyer who, for his day in court, got a string of horses with saddles and all the prospector's outfit, everything the prospector owned. He told of Jack Evans; told of travelling with him.

The people mentioned in the archival papers were early pioneers in our valley and beyond. Their names are preserved on the waterways, Kidprice Lake near Smithers, Evans Creek in the Robson Valley, Cook Creek on the way to Kamloops, and Derr Creek toward Jasper.

When I assembled this material, I realized that I had enough material to reconstruct a tragic episode in British Columbia history. I have done that following as closely as possible the events as recorded. The scene of the shooting is reconstructed from court testimony, as is the involvement of various people. Names of the main characters and many of the minor ones are authentic. *The Golden Era* made no mention of a fight in court, but the climate in the town ensured that one would ensue, if not in the court, then later. I chose the courthouse, and since I chose that setting, I had to imprison two men. Otherwise, the shooting, the evidence, and the testimony are as recorded in the archives.

After I had written for months, I sat looking at the judge's bench book—so many words I couldn't read. I couldn't make sense of it. Are judge's notes, I thought, like doctor's prescriptions, written in Latin? These pages might well have been. I was still frustrated when Ralph Wass, my neighbor, dropped in.

"You're an Englishman," I said. "The judge is an Englishman. What's he saying?" I showed him my problem.

To my surprise, he began to read. "Looks like my dad's writing," he commented.

Problem solved! I soon acquired additional information to insert into the manuscript from beginning to end. As I wrote, I discovered that, as much information as I had, I needed more. I read *Golden Memories* produced by The Golden and District Historic Society. I phoned the Golden and District Museum, explained my project and requested pictures of the Golden of 1899 plus information on the people named in the government records and the newspapers. Colleen Torrence, Curator, dug up information on Griffith, Stipendiary Magistrate, J. Stirrett, acting constable, Dr. Taylor, the doctor who made a journey of nearly four-hundred miles to perform an autopsy, and Thomas O'Brien who was liberally praised for his defence of the accused. She gave me names of descendants of Catherine Conner, the first interpreter, and I phoned them. Colleen sent pictures. But she had no information on Archdeacon McKay, the second interpreter.

The Archdeacon intrigued me. How did he learn Cree? Was he a comfort to the poor widow so far from home and lost in a foreign culture with a language she did not know? When was the Archdeacon bitten with the wandering spirit, and why did he roam? The newspapers had printed several articles recording his travels. He had barely returned from the Klondike when he headed for Tête Jaune Cache.

The Anglican Church Archives in Vancouver had no record of the Archdeacon. I wrote the National Archives in Ottawa, and the archives replied apologizing for a three to four month delay before they could process my request. However, four months later, I received information on McKay's genealogy plus a photocopy of his request for scrip.

In the meantime, I had spent half a day in the Jasper Museum and Archives where I hoped to find further information on the McCaulays. Glenda Cornforth located, for me, papers and books on the history of the Métis of the Jasper area in the late 19th century. Glenda also instructed me on the most likely sources for further information, and at her suggestion, I phoned several archives in Alberta, Saskatchewan, and Manitoba; I travelled to The Glenbow Archives in Calgary.

The name, McCaulay was spelled differently in different documents—McCaulay, Macaulay, Macauley, McAulay and I searched all the above archives under all spellings, but found no information. However, in the Glenbow I found a genealogy, an article published in *The Canadian Cattlemen*, and an autobiography, more than I wanted to know, on the elusive Archdeacon.

In the early summer of 1994 after spending the winter researching and writing, I returned to Victoria to see what further I could find.

I asked to see the file that had been copied for me and the judge's bench book, and I studied these carefully. Mr. McBride again showed me how to use the files to find biographic information, and I found several items about the judge and the Crown counsel. While I was searching for these, Mr. McBride produced records of government expenditures for the year, 1899. Payments made to cover the cost of the trial were there recorded. I now had enough information to reconstruct the murder scene, the weeks before and after, and the preliminary hearings and Supreme Court trial.

By the summer of 1995, an unbelievable amount of information had surfaced. The story of the trapper's family and the prospectors in a remote wilderness was reconstructed; the people of Golden had come to life, but I could not see Adelaide McCaulay in Golden: my attempts to put her there rang hollow.

I was in the garden digging out weeds, fighting off depression, and searching the hidden corners of my mind for inspiration. I heard the phone.

"A box appeared on our doorstep," were the first words that registered. It was Colleen Torrence from the museum at Golden. She knew I would want to see, to examine, the papers from this box.

A few days later when I opened the envelope, I saw folded sheets of antique paper just as Colleen had described. My eyes lighted on a folded sheet. I picked it up and turned it over in my hand.

Marigold yellow, woven linen card—

"*In the Court of Oyer and Terminer and General Gaol Delivery,*" I read. "*The Queen against James Hughes. Order for change of venue.*"

Carefully I opened a sheet of linen paper as thin as onion skin and like new, still, after nearly a century. Judge Drake's signature covered the order of change of venue from County of Cariboo to County of Kootenay. The date was October 31st,

1899. I held it up to the light, *"W T & Co., EXTRA STRONG 3009,"* I read the water mark. I re-folded and replaced it.

I extracted another document, opaque, in a shade of blue we called Queen Elizabeth Blue when I was young. The texture of the paper is similar to the material once, and perhaps still, used for maps, not woven linen but a quality rag. The edges are only slightly frayed and faded. At the top of the page, the lion and the unicorn recline peacefully, backs to the crown. The Attorney-General stamped his approval, July 12, 1899. I read:

> Information and Complaint for an Indictable Offence. CANADA: PROVINCE OF BRITISH COLUMBIA, County of Kootenay. The Information and Complaint of John William Evans taken this ninth day of July, in the year of our Lord one thousand eight hundred and ninety-nine, before the undersigned, one of Her Majesty's Stipendiary Magistrates and for the said County of North East Kootenay, who said that James Hughes did on the twelfth day of June, 1899, on a camp on the Fraser River near the mouth of Swift Current Creek, shoot Alexander McCaulay with intent to kill.
>
> (Signed) John William Evans
>
> Sworn before me the day and year first above mentioned at Donald.
>
> (Signed) J. E. Griffith
>
> STIPENDIARY MAGISTRATE IN AND FOR NORTHERN DIVISION DISTRICT EAST KOOTENAY

Griffith's writing is light and flowing. He used black ink and a fine nib, but Jack Evans signed strongly and squarely with a firm hand. I returned this form to the envelope.

Forms covering deposition of witnesses, statement of the accused, warrant to apprehend, I held them all, all in the same Queen Elizabeth Blue wrappers. However, on these the lion and the unicorn had been alerted and had turned to the crown. They presented a united force.

The depositions of all the witnesses were handwritten by Griffith on lined foolscap. I could decipher his handwriting easily. I had read typed copies for two years and memorized them. I held a page to the light and read *ESPARTO, Best Quality, No. 33.*

I held up another sheet and examined the water mark on it. Britannia sits regally surrounded by an oval frame which is topped with a crown. Within the crown, the cross of the crusader, Richard the Lion-hearted, is twice defined. In one hand Britannia holds her scepter, in the other, her orb. Saint George's cross decorates the shield at her side.

The original handwritten documents allowed glimpses into those courtrooms which had been obscured in the typed copies. The forms and the paper reinforced the knowledge that we were a British colony. Doodling in the judge's bench book suggested the judge's thoughts. When he wrote the Cree word *na moya*, albeit as two words, in the margin, was he trying to bypass the interpreter and understand what Adelaide said? Were the other doodles prompted by his thoughts while he listened to the interpreter and Adelaide converse in Cree?

The newly discovered documents solved many mysteries. I realized that Adelaide, Kid, and Dan left Swift Current Creek with a plan. Dan would interpret Adelaide's speech to the whitemen and interpret the whiteman's world to Adelaide. Information not copied onto the typed sheets allowed me to realized how soon after he entered the courthouse Dan was dismissed from that task. A sentence begun and then crossed out suggested that Dan's testimony wasn't completely recorded. Signatures helped me to form an understanding of the writers. Changes in the signature (when a hand shook, for example) suggested the writer's mood.

Suddenly, I saw that courthouse, bastion of the Empire, emblem of civilization, recently moved to that new town in the Rockies. I saw Adelaide. Dressed in a long dark cotton skirt and long sleeved blouse, she wore moose hide moccasins and leggings. Her long braids were covered with a shawl.

I saw Dan Noyes at her side. Dan's accent, his clothes, even his smell was Indian. His face was white; his features Caucasian. The magistrate and the clerk looked away when he spoke. Dan's years at the mission school had taught him to be humble, to act subserviently, and Adelaide took her cue from him.

Gradually, Adelaide's presence in the court room became clearer, more sharply defined. I could see Adelaide standing before the polished counter; see her pick up the pen as Griffith spoke and Dan translated. Carefully, she made her cross, upright like the one on Alex's grave but less than a centimetre in height.

Then, Adelaide thought about burying Alex. She thought about Dan talking to the whiteman's god. She remembered going back and placing charms for the spirits. No spirits had followed her here into this polished place—not the spirits of the forest, mountain, birds or flowers—none. She put pen to paper and traced a shorter cross over the lines of the first. It looked vaguely like the crucified Christ. Only whiteman's god would come in here.

Glossary

Cree terms:

apsiss – small

astum – come here

keqway – what

kispin ke saigen – if you like me

kohkum – grandmother

Manitou – god

matahikun – scraping knife

mihkehkwun – scraper

mokoman – knife

Moniyaw – whiteman

Moniyaw moya nesokamen – Whiteman did not help me

muqway – nothing

musom – grandfather

namoya – no

napim – husband

Ni nampin mokoman moya misguit – My husband did not carry a big knife.

nistow – brother-in-law (a term sometimes used to indicate a friend who is not a blood relative, but is accepted as family)

nisoh kumakewin – help me

Puga keneso kamoya – We must help him.

Paskshot! Ni napim paskshow ow. – Shot! My husband is shot.

saymuk koshamin – come kiss me

Qwigo! Muqway gesgetum. – That's enough! He knows nothing.

tanehki – why

wihtikow – cannibal spirit

English terms:

camp robber – the gray jay or whisky jack

true bill – bill of indictment. It was the duty of the grand jury to examine the evidence and decide whether enough existed to warrant a trial. If they found enough evidence, they brought a bill of indictment which, at the time, was called a true bill.

Index